VIOLENCE

Understanding, Intervention and Prevention

Ray Braithwaite

RADCLIFFE PROFESSIONAL PRESS

© 1992 Radcliffe Professional Press
15 Kings Meadow, Ferry Hinksey Road, Oxford OX2 0DP

British Library Cataloguing in Publication Data

Braithwaite, Ray
    Violence: understanding, intervention and prevention
    I. Title
    303.62

ISBN 1 870905 92 X

Printed and bound in Great Britain
Typeset by Acorn Bookwork, Salisbury

Contents

This is a workbook designed for anyone who has dealings with members of the public. The exercises contained within this publication although primarily designed for workers in the caring professions are appropriate for use by workers in all fields where aggressive or violent behaviour may occur.

1

Introduction

It is not as easy as it may seem to give a simple, all embracing definition of violence because violence is, I believe, a personal experience. What I consider to be violence may be considered as a normal everyday occurrence by others. One definition I like which takes this into account is that used by the Association of Directors of Social Services, *'Violence is defined as behaviour which produces damaging or hurtful effects physically or emotionally on another person'*.

The importance of this definition is that it recognizes that to have been the subject of violence you need not have suffered a physical assault. This definition allows for the consideration of the effects of emotional damage and accepts that threats, intimidation, verbal abuse, sexual harrassment and racist comments may all be considered as violence if the subject of the abuse has been emotionally harmed.

All forms of violence are intolerable and there can be no excuse for violence of any form. Irrespective of the victims' actions, there is never a valid reason to use an act of violence against another person. Yet violence is prevalent within society. It breaks through the social stratus and occurs in all walks of life. It takes place in the home, in schools and workplaces, in the peace and quiet of the countryside, along a busy road, or in a deserted lane. Violence is a part of life, an unfortunate part, an undesirable part, yet an everyday part of everyone's life. This fact must be accepted by everyone. No longer can you live with the belief that *'it always happens to someone else never to me'*, because if you do maintain that belief, when it does happen you will be doubly damaged as your belief in your own impregnability will lie shattered alongside your damaged body or emotions.

As a social worker, and perhaps too as a man, I always believed I would be able to handle an aggressive situation, and cope with the emotions generated within myself following any such incident.

When I was faced by an aggressive, violent man I could not believe what I did. I froze. No more than that. All my training on how to communicate effectively with another human being meant absolutely nothing. I, like so many others before me, froze. Following the assault I discovered that I was not prepared for the range of emotions which I experienced.

This workbook will help anyone who has to deal with members of the public who may be aggressive or violent. In particular this book provides practical exercises which will help overcome the process of freezing, will help you to deal with aggressive and violent behaviour and to understand and cope with the effects of such behaviour.

Each chapter offers suggestions and advice and may be used by an individual or group of workers.

The advice given comes from a trainer who has had over four years experience of training groups and individuals in methods of handling, defusing and avoiding violent and aggressive behaviour and of considering the effects of such behaviour upon the victim. I have worked in social work for over 16 years and, in compiling this workbook have drawn from personal experience and the experiences of those around me. The ideas, suggestions and solutions offered within this workbook are based upon experience.

RAY BRAITHWAITE
January 1992

2

True or False?

1. **Women are more at risk of violence than men**.
False. Men are more at risk of crime than women, and particularly of violent, street crime.

2. **Old people are more likely to be victims of violence than younger ones**.
False. Young men are the most vulnerable group.

3. **Most people can walk or ride the streets of Great Britain without becoming a victim of violence**.
True. However, commonsense precautions will help make you feel more secure. *See* pages 77–80.

4. **A handbag snatcher will generally hit the victim to take the bag**.
False.

5. **Violence is on the increase**.
? No reliable evidence exists to support or refute this.

6. **Mugging is more common than your car being damaged or something from it being stolen**.
False. The likelihood of being mugged is considerably less.

7. **Most acts of violence are spontaneous**.
False. Most acts of violence require some form of build-up (*see* pages 35–61).

8. **A personal alarm will summon help**.
? In an exercise carried out by the consumer magazine *Which* the only response to a personal alarm set off in 13 different places was from people who thought their car was being stolen. However, *see* page 98.

9. **Generally, most people believe that violence is something which happens to someone else and not to themselves**.
True.

10. **Young men are the most likely victims of violence**.
True.

11. **Most of the crime on railways and the Underground is directed against property**.
True.

12. **You are far more likely to have your property damaged or stolen than be injured in a violent crime**.
True.

3

Definitions of Violence

Violence is a very personal issue. Like pain, some can experience it at a greater level than others, before it has an effect.

It is important to consider this, as within any group of workers there could be a number of different definitions of what constitutes violence. Within the group this could give rise to there being a number of acceptable levels of violence. One worker may, for example, feel it is acceptable to be sworn at by a client while another, in the same working group, may consider this unacceptable. Similarly, a threat may be treated by one worker as a normal part of that client's functioning; while another may consider threats to be over-stepping the line.

Imagine the effects upon the client when workers within the same group apply different standards and give different messages about the same behaviour.

Consistency of approach and of messages given are fundamental elements within any form of client contact. However, this consistency cannot be established if individual workers, within the same group, department or agency, have varying definitions of violence.

Exercise

1. What forms of client behaviour do you tolerate in the performance of your job?

2. What is your definition of violence?

3. What forms of client behaviour do your colleagues tolerate?

4. What are your colleagues' definitions of violence?

5. Does your agency/team have a unified definition of what is considered to be acceptable and unacceptable client behaviour?

6. What sanctions empower this definition?

A number of basic definitions exist. The Concise Oxford Dictionary describes violence as: *'Violence, n. Quality of being violent; violent conduct or treatment; outrage, injury, as was compelled to use . . . unlawful exercise of physical force, intimidation by exhibition of this.'*

Other definitions for violence include: *'the application of force, severe threat or serious abuse, by members of the public towards people arising out of the course of their work whether or not they are on duty'*;

and it includes:

'severe verbal abuse or threat where this is judged likely to turn into actual violence; serious or persistent harassment (including racial or sexual harassment); threat with a weapon; major or minor injury; fatalities'. Violence to Staff: Report of the DHSS Advisory Committee on Violence to Staff. HMSO (1988).

'Violence is purposeful or reactive behaviour, including threats with or without weapons, spitting, physical injury and other sorts of behaviour intended to produce damaging or hurtful effects, physically or emotionally, on anyone'. Guidance to Staff on Violence by Clients. Cheshire Social Services Department.

'Any incident in which an employee is abused, threatened or assaulted by a member of the public in circumstances arising out of the course of his or her employment'. Violence to Staff. Health and Safety Executive. (1989)

'Violence is behaviour which produces damaging or hurtful effects physically or emotionally on other people. This definition is not limited simply to physical assault but permits the inclusion of equally distressing and intimidating verbal aggression'. Guidelines and Recommendations to Employers on Violence against Employees. Association of Directors of Social Services (1987).

Everyone has their own definition of violence. You know when the line has been stepped over, when you have been damaged either physically or emotionally. You know the difference between a client, or colleague, who makes frequent use of swear words or threatening gestures as a part of their natural method of communicating and another who is actually attempting to damage you in some way. You also (hopefully) have an appreciation of yourself and can identify that on some days you can deal with and take more than on other days. However, the danger in this individualistic and subjective definition is that the inconsistent response you then give your client(s) can vary from day to day and from worker to worker. A standard definition for violence and a standard response to it needs to be identified within each and every place of work where violence is likely to be experienced.

Exercise

1. Discuss with your colleagues what is likely to happen to a client who exhibits violence in a waiting area:
   - in a police station?
   - in your workplace?

2. Do your clients know what level of behaviour is acceptable and unacceptable within your work environment?

3. Identify what your feelings are regarding a standard response within your workplace to acts of violence.

4

The Effects of Violence

Violence damages both physically and emotionally – emotional damage being the hardest to deal with. There are a number of reasons for this:
1. It cannot be seen.
2. It is an admission of failure on your part if you acknowledge it.
3. It happens so often that you become hardened to it.
4. You believe, that because your work deals with other people's emotions, that means you can deal with your own, but you never do.
5. You shelve the emotion to deal with at a later date which seldom arrives.
6. You deny the situation has any emotional effect upon you.
7. It would not look good on your record if you say you have been 'emotionally damaged'.
8. It's dangerous to consider the emotional effects upon yourself too often. If you did you'd probably not be able to do the job.
9. It's part of the agency/team culture – 'other people don't mention it so I don't think I should'.
10. You take it as part of the job.
11. It's what you're trained for.
12. You've just got to cope with it – there's no time for anything else.
13. It's a sign of weakness.
14. It may effect the way others view you if you admit to emotional harm.
15. It's all right for a woman to feel such things, but not a man.

Exercise

QUESTIONNAIRE
1. Have you ever faced violence in the performance of your duties?   Yes / No
   If yes, how many times?   1–3 / 4–7 / More than 7

2. Do you feel your agency helped or hindered you following the incident(s)?
Incident
a)

b)

c)

d)

How?
a)

b)

c)

d)

3. What helped, or would have helped, when you were subjected to violence?

4. What can be done for colleagues who have experienced violence?

5. What do you do for your colleagues who have been subjected to violence?

6. How do your colleagues perceive this?

Please discuss your findings with your colleagues/agency.

The immediate physical effects

When afraid, for example, when you are confronted by violent or aggressive behaviour, a number of physical changes can take place within your body. These physical changes include:
- accelerated heart rate
- increased blood pressure
- shallow and rapid breathing
- increased flow of acids and digestive juices
- digestive movements cease
- raised blood glucose level
- blood diverted from internal organs of the body
- increased peripheral circulation of the blood
- tensed and contracted muscles of the trunk and limbs and this may cause some uncontrolled movement or shaking in knees, arms and finger tips
- increased production of adrenaline, noradrenaline, cortisone, endorphins and other hormones
- panoramic or tunnel vision develops as the pupils expand or contract
- increased sensory input giving the impression that events are slowed down or speeded up
- auditory blocking or selective hearing

- tensing of the neck and shoulder muscles reducing the flow of saliva to the throat
- dryness of the throat and vocal cords leading to a quavering voice
- tightening of the facial muscles promoting an oppressed feeling
- uncontrolled quivering around the lips
- a nervous 'tic' about the eyes, forehead or neck.

The immediate emotional effects

The emotional processes which you go through at the same time may include:
- anger
- surprise
- fear
- hostility
- disbelief
- self-doubt
- embarrassment
- shock
- guilt
- insecurity
- vulnerability
- violation
- attraction
- repulsion
- anxiety.

Individuals react to violence and fear in their own way and the effects of violence upon each person vary. However, with the possibility of a combination of any of the above taking place in you, within the concentrated time period of the incident of violence (and that could be a mere split second), it is not difficult to imagine that your body and your emotions will need some time to readjust.

Exercise

Imagine a violent situation in which you were involved.
1. Note down the events beforehand under these two headings:

What were you doing?   How did you feel?

2. Now consider the situation itself. Think through the events. Allow them to unroll. Note them down. Go over them purposefully.

3. What physical sensations do you remember experiencing?

4. What emotions do you remember experiencing?

Post-traumatic Incident Syndrome

The most common effects of violent incidents experienced by the victim/worker have been categorized under the title Post-traumatic Incident Syndrome. These effects can begin to be felt within a few days of an incident taking place. However, there may be delayed reactions months, even years later. Reactions may not catch up with you until you reduce the pressure of work, make some change, take a holiday or even retire.

It is estimated that about 80% of individuals who experience violence will experience one or more of these syptoms and of these, about 80% will overcome the effects successfully.

There are five possible symptoms which make up post-traumatic incident syndrome:

- performance guilt
- focused resentment or anger
- reconstruction anxiety
- irritability
- loss of motivation.

Performance guilt

Although there may have been nothing you could have done to prevent the incident from taking place, all too commonly you will examine your own performance critically and blame yourself for being there, or for not handling the situation well. This can build up into a critical examination:

1. The 'if only I'd' synopsis – *'if only I'd not said or done that'*; or *'if only I'd said or done something else'*.
2. An inability to blame the person who has damaged you because you categorize them as vulnerable – *'he's an old man . . . a child in care . . . mentally ill'*.
3. The quality of 'understanding' – *'I can understand why s/he did it s/he's had an awful life'*.
4. Your need for a reason for the behaviour – *'s/he wasn't getting at me, it was the system s/he wanted to damage really'*.

With this process taking place, it becomes possible to identify how the focus of blame has been gradually moved from the perpetrator to yourself. There is another reason for this self-blame and that comes from the insecurity experienced following the incident. Before the violence you felt you knew your capabilities. You felt reasonably secure in your knowledge-base and your skills. You may have had years of experience and of practising these skills. Following the incident this security, this knowledge-base, this experience is stripped from you and you are left floundering, wondering what you did wrong. Having experienced great emotional and physical changes for which you were unprepared, having had a routine day shattered with little or no warning, self-doubt and questions about any and every aspect of your existence and your concepts begin.

Focused resentment or anger *(see* also page 17)

As you will have difficulty in feeling angry with the person who has damaged you (*see* above) that anger and resentment has to go somewhere. One thing you can do with the resentment and anger is redirect it towards someone closer to you and that may be your line manager, the 'department', a friend, colleague or loved one. This is characterized in such expressions as: *'You sent me. You should have known'*, *'if you'd turned up on time it wouldn't have happened'*, *'it's the Department's fault for not . . .'* etc.

Resentment and anger are feelings which many people are uneasy with and have difficulty in expressing honestly and openly. How many of you can, for example, acknowledge that you are angry and express your feelings to the person concerned in a manner which allows for shared discussion? Feelings of anger and resentment do show themselves however in different circumstances and in a variety of forms. When you are angry how many of you will:

- go quiet and/or keep quiet for a time – maybe for days
- simmer for days before taking action
- count up/make a list of the items which cause the anger
- blow-up bringing in all the items on your list (and some of these can be years old!)
- feel hurt when actually you are outraged
- bury your feelings in your work
- determine how to get your own back in an underhand manner
- hold on to the anger
- take the anger out on someone else
- take the anger out on yourself – drink/migraine/stomach problems etc
- take the anger out on the furniture/the car/the door/the cat!
- consider who you are really angry with and how angry you feel
- engage others in a conversation focusing on the 'bad' points of the person concerned
- acknowledge that anger is what you are feeling
- forgive the person
- become overtly polite and covertly destructive
- try to illicit people onto 'your side'
- allow the anger to go from you, to no longer have such an effect, or such power over you.

Exercise

1. What do you do with your anger?

2. Which of the above list of behaviours are constructive and which are destructive?

3. If someone is feeling angry with you would you like the opportunity of discussing this with them in a calm way?

   Provide a list of alternatives which you might prefer the person who is angry with you to legitimately take.

4. Make a list of those people you are angry with.

5. What can you do about this?

6. How can you stop your anger from damaging you?

Reconstruction anxiety

In view of the physical changes and emotional processes you can experience when afraid the imprinted memory of the event can stay with you.

Exercise

1. Consider a violent incident in the past in which you were involved. How much detail can you recall?

2. Do you have the same recall of details for other events which occurred in your life at the same time?

The imprinted memory of the event can be triggered off at unexpected times. This 'trigger' will cause you to reconstruct the episode, or perhaps a particular part of it.

A trigger may be a sight, a sound, a smell, a sensation or a similar set of circumstances; and, with the trigger, the sensations which flooded through your body at the time of the event may happen again. You may re-experience physical reactions similar to those which existed at the time of the event; sweating palms, trembling knee, quivering lip, hands shaking and so on, combined with the over-riding emotion(s) which also flooded into your senses at that time.

Reconstruction anxiety can occur at any time and in any place as the association of ideas, events or feelings are made. Often it can occur in your sleep, coming in the form of dreams or racing through your mind just as you fall asleep or begin to wake.

Irritability

Taken for granted reality can be stripped away by a violent incident, so too can your belief in yourself and your abilities. Trust in your colleagues, friends and society may be questioned, as well as your beliefs and values. Personal security may be lost and you may think that you are never going to be 'safe' again.

These internal doubts, questions and re-ordering of assumptions may show themselves in an outward display of irritability. Combine this questioning and self-doubt with the knowledge that your body needs time to adjust to the physical and emotional changes experienced, and it is hardly surprising that you become irritable not only with yourself and colleagues but also with friends and loved ones. Being the subject of this weeks' office gossip also does little to reduce the feelings of doubt, insecurity and loss that can be expressed as irritability.

Loss of motivation

'I don't get paid enough to take this, I'll turn up, just do the job . . . won't put my heart into it any more – I've learned my lesson . . . they don't care about me why should I bother about them' are all expressions of loss of motivation from people who had previously been very committed to the work they were doing.

The veneer of personal security has been removed. You may feel threatened, unsupported, unreasonably uncomfortable and vulnerable. You may experience a disabling fear that as it has happened once it could all too easily happen again, only next time it could be worse.

The basis upon which you entered your chosen profession has been shattered. The self-critical questioning and self-doubt has begun. A loss of motivation may cause you to pull out of situations involving risk taking, seeking not to confront or challenge, refusing to allow for the legitimate expression of any anger. In some cases loss of motivation leads to a search for a more secure, less hazardous career.

What can you do about Post-traumatic Incident Syndrome?

Performance guilt

- Do not duck the issue of feeling angry with the person who has damaged you.
- Identify that it is difficult to acknowledge extremely punitive feelings.
- Be gentle with yourself.
- Remind yourself you are not a magician, you cannot legislate for every situation. Maybe you could improve your performance but irrespective of this there is no excuse for violence.
- Stop blaming yourself.
- Blame the person who has damaged you.

Focused resentment or anger

- Acknowledge that this is how you are feeling.
- Claim and accept any personal expression of this feeling as your behaviour.
- Consider who you are feeling resentful or angry towards. Be specific, detail the item(s) or

incidents and consider the depths of feeling you have. This will help to develop a feeling of power over the emotion.

- Actively choose to do something constructive about your feelings. Think about either approaching the person concerned to discuss your feeling(s) or if this is impossible or unviable, giving up your feelings. Being prepared to let go, to stop holding on to the feelings, cancelling the charges against others and/or yourself will help you to increase personal power and effectiveness.
- Remember that forgiveness is a powerful concept but it is not easy to practise.

Reconstruction anxiety

- Take time for yourself. When you feel the time is right, allow yourself to think of the incident(s), either alone, or with someone.
- Talk about the incident, either with a colleague, a friend or alone. Actually say the words aloud, so that you can hear them. They can sound more real, and perhaps less frightening than ideas rushing through your mind and once verbally expressed somehow become more tangible and more able to be dealt with.
- If you are unable to talk about the incident think about writing it down, or drawing pictures about it.
- Do as little or as much as you choose.
- Take your time, a return to equilibrium will come; it will take longer for some than for others and some may require professional counselling.
- Do not be afraid of seeking counselling. To identify and to address personal development needs is a strength.

These actions will allow you to begin to take charge of the anxiety, to bring it back within your control.

Irritability

- Be aware that this could happen and share this awareness with those around you (before an incident if possible).
- Share the way you are feeling with family, friends and colleagues following an incident. They will see it anyway but will not always know whether they should mention it fearing that they 'may make it worse'.

Loss of motivation

- Consider your systems of staff support and how these can be improved.
- Following an incident do not automatically expect that you will be able to resume work at the same level, some people may, some may not.
- Consider the nurturing required for someone damaged physically or emotionally and apply the same thoughts to yourself.
- Think of methods of getting yourself back into the job.
- Have limited expectations which are achievable.
- Take your time.

Exercise

1. What are the immediate needs of a colleague who has experienced violence?

2. Describe the system of staff support you would like to see in your office and the system of staff support which presently exists.
   - Ideal staff support system

   - Present system

3. What are the major differences between these systems?

4. What can be done to ensure adequate staff support occurs within your office?

Effects on staff working in residential and day care

The effects of a violent incident on staff in a residential or day care establishment can be far reaching. Within such a setting clients and staff repeatedly come together and it becomes imperative that ways of reducing the likelihood of a violent incident taking place are considered and that the effects following a violent episode and possible ways of reducing these, are examined. The effects can include the following:

- lowering of staff morale
- team and/or self-criticism
- loss of security at a practical level and/or an emotional level
- anger released at clients
- frustration at the lack of available and viable sanctions
- tiredness
- lack of confidence in self and system.

Possible solutions for these could be as follows.

Effect	Solution
1. Lowering of staff morale	• Support. • Reassurance. • Supervision in a group for support. • Individual supervision to examine how the worker is/how situation was handled/how potential violence may be reduced in the future/time taken to allow for the feelings about incident to be explored. • Supportive management presence. • Time together relaxing, having a good time as a staff group.
2. Team-self-criticism	• Reassurance for each other. • Give space, time and understanding. • Focus upon successes. • Acknowledge that everyone is only human.
3. Loss of security (practical and emotional)	• Ensure building is secure. Check everything is OK at potentially critical times – mealtimes, admission etc. Make sure there are enough staff around at such times. Check with colleagues. • Issue personal alarms to staff. • Let clients know you are human too and can be afraid but can still carry on and handle the situation. • Take time to rebuild personal esteem – let others know your decision-making process may be slowed down.
4. Anger released at client	• Explain to client why and what is happening. • Apologize where necessary.
5. Frustration at lack of sanctions available	• Restate the policy. • Restate the way you work. • Rationally examine the sanctions available. • Consider the methods of imposing sanctions. • Identify acceptable and unacceptable levels of behaviour and rules to enforce this. • Ensure all staff use same criteria.
6. Tiredness	• Staff to be aware of colleagues' moods/state of being and compensate for each other. • Ask and tell. Don't expect colleagues to be mind readers – let other people know your mood/state. • Discuss what can be done – what action can be taken to reduce levels of tiredness among staff.

Effect	**Solution**
7. Lack of confidence in self and system	• Rota changes to ensure shifts are as strong as possible – this may mean extra staff or overtime in short term. • Regular staff meetings used for support. • Take time to rebuild confidence. Do not expect to cope at same level or with same workload. • Look after yourself. • Remind yourself you are important. • Learn to give support and encouragement to peers and management and to take it in return.

Exercise

1. Identify what could be (or are) the effects of a violent incident taking place within your establishment.

2. What will be possible solutions to redress these effects?

Debriefing counselling

Colleagues can offer debriefing counselling to anyone who has experienced violence. The following model may help to clarify some of the confusion experienced by victims and may reduce the possible effects described. Although this model can be used by any colleague, it is expected that the person making use of the approach will be sensitive to the needs of the victim, will not comment upon the information being received, will offer reinforcements (head nods and verbal prompts) and will keep the information received confidential. If you find that you are uncomfortable with discussing emotional issues it will be more difficult for you to make use of this model to help a colleague.

It is also possible for the victim to make use of this model without the assistance of someone else. This is particularly useful for those individuals who are unable to share intense emotional information with others.

Part I: Before the incident (*see* model)

1. Colleague asks victim: *'What was happening before the incident?'* (It is the specific facts, not emotions and not impressions but facts which are to be focused upon initially.)
2. Colleague asks victim: *'How were you feeling at this time?'* (By drawing the victim's attention to the feelings being experienced before the incident it is possible to begin to view the changes in feelings as part of a process).
3. Colleague asks victim: *'How were you expressing those feelings?'* (This gives the victim the opportunity to become aware of the physiological changes which took place within him/her.)

Part II: During the incident

Repeat the above questions focusing on the time period while the incident was taking place: *'Tell me what was happening, the actual facts, during the incident,'* *'How did this make you feel?'*, *'How did you express those feelings?'*, *'Were there any conscious body mannerisms? Any unconscious ones?'*

Part III: Immediately following the incident

Ask the victim to consider the same questions focusing this time on the time period immediately following the incident: *'Tell me what was happening, the actual facts, immediately after the incident,'* *'How did this make you feel?'*, *'How did you express those feelings?'* etc.

Part IV: Now with hindsight

Finally ask the victim to consider a similar set of questions about the episode, this time referring to the present: *'With hindsight have the facts changed?'*, *'Have you changed?'*, *'What are your feelings about this?'*, *'How do you express these feelings?'*

Exercise: Debriefing model (complete from left to right)

	What were the specific facts which you remember	How were you feeling?	How were you expressing those feelings?
Before the incident			
While the incident was happening			
Immediately following the incident			
Now with hindsight			

It is difficult to estimate the time that may be needed for debriefing someone who has experienced violence. The length of time required will vary from person to person. However, a guideline is to use this model in three or perhaps a maximum of four one hour sessions in order to give the individual the necessary time, space and attention required. Some people will not need so much time, others will need more. This model will not always be appropriate. Some people will not respond to this approach, some people will not want to and some people will be unable to. A small, but perhaps significant number may require professional counselling assistance. This model is offered, not to replace other interventions but in addition to them.

The needs of victims of violence

This is by no means a complete or comprehensive list; it is a guideline to provide some ideas and to stimulate some thought on the subject.
- Understanding.
- Comfort and warmth.
- To be encouraged to talk.
- To share their experience with others.

- Access to others who have experienced violence and adjusted.
- Someone to take over. To take immediate control. To make immediate decisions.
- To regain a normal pattern of behaviour.
- To overcome feelings of loss of security, guilt at surviving, self-blame, self-doubt.
- To be able to relax and sleep.
- Time to re-adjust.
- Time to explore the incident.
- Time to explore a way forward.
- To be reacted to positively by colleagues and management.
- Space to recover.
- To examine the emotional content of the situation.
- A clear choice of future contact with the aggressor.
- Information about compensation, insurance, legal systems.
- Support.
- Not to be interrogated.

5

Anger

Holding on to anger

Anger is a very powerful emotion. So powerful that many people are unwilling to allow it to dissipate – failing to let it go, holding on to it, nurturing it and allowing it to grow. Sometimes you can hold on to your anger for years, often with the reason for its existence being forgotten or becoming so confused with the passage of time that it becomes impossible to find any resolution to it.

By holding on to your anger you can set in motion a part of the process which leads to embitterment and disillusionment. When angry do you:

- keep quiet?
- feel hurt?
- shrug it off?
- go for a swim?
- discuss it with composure?
- store it up?
- take it home?
- work out where it comes from?
- express it assertively?
- take it out on someone else?
- decide the world is against you?
- avoid the aggressor in future?

- blow up?
- get depressed?
- deny you are harmed?
- kick a football?
- become irritable?
- get headaches?
- drink?
- simmer for days?
- draw colleagues onto 'your side'?
- kick the cat?
- walk away?
- maintain a cool dislike for the aggressor.

The above are all possible ways of dealing with your anger. However, not many of you will actually devise an active strategy for dealing with your anger. It is more common to let your anger deal with you!

Case history 1

I was working as a social worker in a local authority. One of my jobs involved running a club for the recovering mentally ill. The club met regularly on Thursday evenings for different social activities. Unfortunately, one of the members, 'Tim', had begun to show signs of recurring illness and had been refusing contact with his doctors and social worker for the previous two weeks. One of his symptoms involved a belief that he was in love with one of the female members at the club and he viewed me as a competitor for her affections. He had given up his lodgings and begun to sleep rough but still attended the club regularly. Here, he had begun to become verbally destructive but it was only when he actually threatened me that I banned him from attending the club until he had seen his consultant.

It was growing dark as I made my way the following Thursday evening to a local café, where I intended to eat, before going on to open the club. The road was busy with people going home from work. As I reached the doorway of the café I caught some movement out of the corner of my eye. I turned in time to see a fist swinging towards my head. My adrenalin raced and events seemed to take on an unrealistic quality as everything slowed down. I moved to one side. The fist hit my shoulder knocking me to the ground. My mind told me not to stay on the floor and I immediately sprang up to face my attacker who was so surprised he ran off. I began to shake as I entered the café and over a coffee tried to understand what had just happened. The assailant was a complete stranger. It didn't make sense.

I reported the incident to the police who took copious notes and agreed to tour the area later keeping a lookout for the man. I must have still been in shock when I opened the club later that night but still went ahead with the night's activities putting the previous events out of my mind.

The following week I was accompanied to the café by one of the other club helpers. As we sat at a table my colleague told me that 'Tim' was outside walking up and down with two other men. I recognized one of them as my assailant from last week. I tried to drink my coffee without spilling any as my colleague went to ask the proprietor if he had a telephone we could use. He returned to explain that there was not a telephone on the premises just as 'Tim' entered the cafe.

'Tim' walked straight past us into the kitchen where he picked up a carving knife before walking back into the seating area. His two friends were outside close to the door. The nearest telephone was about a 100 yards away and the police station about a half a mile. I told my colleague I was going to telephone the police and asked him to wait to see if they followed me before he went to fetch the police.

As casually as I could I walked to the door, opened it and stepped outside. 'Tim' shouted 'Get him!'. I ran so fast I was past the two outside before they had chance to move. I was terrified and hid behind a small wall. People were still walking home and driving past. Everything was normal, yet I knew I was being hunted and I was terrified. I remember trying to control my panting breath which sounded like thunder in my ears and I was convinced 'Tim' and his mates would hear me any moment. After a few moments, no more, yet it seemed like an eternity, I looked over the wall. They were not in sight. I half walked, half crawled to the telephone box and called the police. They were under-staffed that evening and asked me if I felt I could walk around to them, 'After all, it's still quite light and there are plenty of people around.' I felt so foolish. Yet that walk to the police station was like a nightmare. My heart was pounding and my legs shook beneath me as I anticipated being attacked any moment.

It took some weeks and another attack where my glasses were smashed after he hit me over the head with a bottle before we were finally in court. He got two years for assault. His comrades were also sentenced. I went home feeling totally unsatisfied. Two years was not enough for what he had done to me! He had made me feel fear. He had made me feel hate. Two years was not enough for stripping me of my security, for changing the perception I had of myself, of the universe. Before these incidents I was secure in my knowledge. I knew how to deal with people. I had been doing it for years. I knew that I was a skilled worker. But now, following the assaults, that veneer of security and knowledge and that belief in my skills had been shattered and 'they' had done it to me. They had taken my peaceful existence and destroyed it and I wasn't about to let them get away with it that easily. Two years was not enough! I hated him and his friends and not just them.

My anger permeated into my work until I began to distrust and dislike most of the people I was working with. I held on to my anger. I wouldn't let it go, yet the person who had damaged me was in prison. His colleagues were in prison and I likewise was in a prison of my own making (the imprisonment which comes from allowing an event to go on affecting you, to continue to damage you long after it has occurred). I was turning my anger towards him on to all mentally ill people, on to the job I was doing, on to the people I worked with and eventually onto myself.

It was only after I realized this that I understood the need to actively do something with the anger I still held. If I didn't do something constructive with my anger I knew it would continue to destroy me. Ultimately I knew I would become so damaged by it that I would cease to function in a job which until then I had gained much satisfaction from.

1. Identify how the victim could have responded to the anger he still had.

2. What could he have done with the anger which would have stopped him from being damaged by it?

In case history 1 the only person the victim was damaging by holding on to the anger was himself. Yet there are a number of things that can be done so that anger no longer has such a hold. To, in effect, stop the anger from continuing to damage you after you have already been damaged by the aggressor.

Always remember that anger is a powerful force and emotion. So powerful, in fact, that you might want to keep hold of it. You might not want to look for ways to allow it to dissipate or to make use of strategies to begin to regain control over it. Some may simply want to experience it or hold on to it for as long as possible, others may view it as a motivator. Anger is a powerful tool if used constructively, but a dangerous weapon if you allow yourself to be controlled and influenced by it.

A strategy for dealing with anger

1. You must decide that you want to do something to address your anger. This means you must think that the time is right and make an active decision to deal with the anger which you hold within you.
2. You need to spend time identifying the specifics. Who are you angry with and why? Remember that with anger you often carry over the emotion from one situation or from one person to another. Often you will dump a lot of anger on one person when in fact that anger may belong somewhere else altogether.
3. Be as clear with yourself as possible and identify how angry you are feeling and over what exactly.
4. Consider the range of emotions you are experiencing in relation to the situation or person and identify which of these emotions is anger. Are you for example, feeling frustrated with your boss when the support he should be providing is not forthcoming, but cannot tell him because he is such a 'nice guy'? Do you feel protective towards him because he is failing or under a lot of pressure? Itemize the range of emotions you are experiencing.
5. Decide how angry you are feeling. Are you mildly irritated by the person or do you feel like strangling them? By analysing the depth of the emotion you can develop a sense of personal power over it rather than allowing it to continue to have power over you. You can also separate the anger out into manageable portions and help to halt the dumping process whereby any anger you feel about another person or situation becomes enmeshed with that which you are already feeling.
6. Acknowledge the anger as *your* emotion and own it. Although you may feel it has been created by another, anger is an emotion and as such is *your* feeling. It is up to you to identify it as such. Once you claim the anger as your feeling you can begin to reduce the power it holds simply by acknowledging it as a feeling and one of your range of emotions.
7. Determine a strategy to deal with it. Three strategies for dealing with personal anger are:

- Approaching the person with whom you feel angry and asking if you can talk to them about your feeling. '*I feel angry with you, can I talk to you about this?*' is not as easy as it sounds. However, if you can do this you will be able to discuss your feelings in a rational manner and give the other person the opportunity to state their point of view. Alternatively, you may give the other person more ammunition to use against you. '*Good, I want you to feel angry!*'. However if this is the case, you are in a better position to make a more realistic appraisal of that individual – you know they are what previously you could only assume them to be, people not worthy of your efforts, your friendship, your trust etc. and you will respond to them in the future using this information.
- Letting the anger dissipate. Sometimes it is impossible to approach the person for whatever reason: they may have moved away, or died, or the person's nature may be such that you may be once again damaged simply by trying to deal with it in this way. Yet your feelings of anger still persist.

  At these times it becomes necessary to consider the damage this anger is causing you and to determine a strategy which will help relieve or reduce this damage. One such strategy involves explaining out loud to yourself what effects holding this anger in are having upon you. Once this has been acknowledged you can then move on to the next stage and this involves making a statement out loud that you choose to be no longer damaged by this anger. The words '*I will not allow this anger to hurt me any more*', can be very therapeutic but do not come easily and may need repeating a number of times in the seclusion and privacy of your room before you actually begin to accept that this is, in fact, the case.

Think about letting it go, and giving it up. Think about getting the words from your mind and placing them in the air so that they actually become more tangible, so that you can actually hear what they sound like.

There are other alternatives to consider which are equally valid and which will replace this process if you do not feel comfortable with it. Some people write down their experiences and find that this helps. Others draw their experiences, play the piano or walk under trees and at times when they are feeling tranquil will then actively think about their anger, their rage or outrage and acknowledge this either inwardly and privately or outwardly making a declaration that now is the time for them to begin to allow the anger to go; now is the time to halt the process of allowing their feelings to continue to damage them. Other people may seek counselling and increasingly employers are looking at the provision of a counsellor available for their staff as part of a staff welfare scheme.

- Forgiving. For many this concept may not be an easy one to accept. It is not easy to forgive someone whose actions have caused so much pain. However, the concept of forgiveness is in itself a strong element which empowers the individual.

Exercise

1. Identify what you do with your anger.

2. Decide which actions you employ are potentially healthy and which are potentially unhealthy.

---

8. Be gentle with yourself. Remind yourself that you are an enabler not a magician. Remember too, that occasionally no matter how skilful you are and irrespective of what you do you can still experience violence. There are those people who are going to damage you and who will not be or cannot be avoided, or handled. You may be damaged not because of any inability, not because of lack of skill but simply because sometimes people do not, cannot or will not respond to your interactions. Fortunately, they are few in number but they do exist.

Exercise

Think of a recent situation/occasion in your life which caused you to feel angry, resentful or annoyed.

1. Briefly write down the circumstances.

2. About whom did you feel this anger/resentment/annoyance? (Name names)

3. How intense was this feeling?

4. What did you do with this feeling?

5. How intense is it still?

6. What do you now need to do with the feeling?

7. What were/are/could be the outcomes of your action(s)?

Expressing anger constructively

Consider the following as a checklist for expressing anger, resentment and/or annoyance constructively.

1. Use statements which are non-evaluative.
2. Ensure statements are descriptive and refer to the incident concerned.
3. Ensure statements are about the feeling which belongs to you.
4. Try to keep statements about *what* not *why*.
5. Remember the feeling is almost always about self-disclosure. Sharing the feeling(s) generated within yourself by the behaviour makes it an interpersonal event. It permits you to give and receive *feedback* and enters you into 'open' discussion with the other person.
6. The expression of anger has been found to be useful when it is:

- **Specific**. Individual items are raised and considered, but because of the individuality of each they may be kept separate from issues of belief and/or principle. The issues are raised in terms of the behaviour concerned and the feeling such behaviour created or gave rise to within yourself.
- **Usable**. You need to judge that the person receiving the information can do something about it; or that the information is such that it may be used and/or acted upon; and that it is given in a manner which *allows* it to be acted upon. It is the behaviour which may be commented upon not the person.
- **Asked for**. Or at least expected. Discussion which is requested is more likely to promote change than imposed comments.
- **Immediate**. Or as soon as possible following an event, remember people do forget.
- **Checked out**. Perceptions of events vary from one person to another so it is crucial that your perceptions of the event are checked out – you may have got it wrong.
- **Clean**. Not given couched in aggressive terms.
- **Honest and congruent**. Statements must be consistent with actual feelings about the person's behaviour. Remember you may carry over emotions from one event and dump it on to someone else, or you may lump all of your emotion together and use the opportunity to bring it all to the fore.

7. Beware of statements like '*I think it would be good for you to know*'.
8. Even if you forget the constructive expression of anger technique remember that an honest, sincere statement of the way you feel is much more helpful in moving your relationship(s) forward than keeping hold of your anger and allowing it to influence your relationship(s).
9. Always consider your motivation – is this really to be an expression of your true feelings or merely a chance to get your own back?
10. Own your own feelings. Remember no-one is responsible for the way you feel. Irrespective of the actions of other people *this is your emotion*. Acknowledge it as such and be determined to do something positive with it, not to get your own back, not for the benefit of someone else but simply and most importantly, for the benefit of yourself.
11. Remember that you may not be able to change anyone or any situation *but* you can change the way you feel about them. You can reduce the emotional investment within the situation. You can reassess the way that you view the issue.
12. Conflicts expressed in terms of belief or principle are harder to manage. Try to break the issue(s) down into identifiable, manageable parts and address each part separately.

Anger summary

- Takes many forms.
- Identify what you are feeling.
- Identify the depth of the feeling.
- Identify against whom the anger is felt.
- Own your own feeling.
- Ask yourself, is it placed where it belongs?
- Do not take it out on just anyone including yourself.
- Do something constructive with the feeling.
- Stop it from continuing to damage you.
- It is a powerful emotion or tool.
- If expressed constructively it can enhance personal growth and improve interpersonal functioning.
- If ignored it can damage you.
- It can be deskilling.
- It can be managed.

6

Non-verbal Signs and Signals

Cultural and ethnic differences

Outlined in this chapter are some of the ways people from various ethnic backgrounds may express themselves both verbally and non-verbally so that potential areas of possible communication misperception can be avoided.

There are too many ethnic variables to become fully aware of all the differences which exist in ways of expressing feelings. However, if you are to meet someone from a different cultural background, even if only infrequently, commonsense dictates that you make yourself as aware as possible of the ways that person may communicate both verbally and through their body language. Before your meeting discuss your expectations or experiences with members from the various ethnic groups which exist within your community. If possible ask your client about their behaviour, attend a racial awareness training course, find out if you have a colleague(s) from the same ethnic background and discuss it with them. Ask, do not assume.

But if you are in any doubt about your safety simply because you do not know about this person's cultural norm for expressing feelings, **or** if you fear that the person to whom you are talking may be becoming violent, **leave**. You can always repair any damage you feel you may have done to your relationship at a later date. You can return, perhaps after obtaining information about this person's culturally accepted ways of expressing themselves. You are the important person. Do not stay assuming that it will be all right. It only has to be not all right *once*.

Indicators of aggression

Few forms of aggressive or violent behaviour are spontaneous. There are, of course, exceptions to this rule. However, with regard to violence and aggression which you meet on a day to day basis the exception will be rare.

From behavioural studies it can be shown that there a number of useful signs which may indicate that aggressive behaviour is possible. By remaining aware of these verbal and non-verbal signs and signals you can:
- avoid the aggressor
- determine a strategy to approach or deal with the aggressor/situation
- make use of the signals yourself to reduce the possibility of, or defuse the aggression
- ensure that you do not escalate the situation with your own body signals.

Exercise

The following exercise highlights many of the non-verbal indications taking place within all forms of communication. It may be used by teams or groups to consider, at an experiential level, the messages you give and receive with body language.

Within the group one person is required to run the exercise. This person gives a card to everyone else present. On each card is one statement. Participants are requested to read the card they have received but to keep the information secret until the conclusion of the exercise.

On the cards the previously written individual statements will include:

- You do not like your partner / Your partner has been spreading malicious rumours about you
- You are very fond of your partner / You idolize your partner
- Your partner has been drinking and is unpredictable / Your partner is likely to be distressed
- You are to give your partner the sack / You have some extremely good news to give your partner
- You are attracted to your partner / You feel sexually harrassed by your partner
- You feel superior to your partner / You have been let down by your partner once too often and are going to confront them about this
- You want to make a good impression on your partner, and so on.

The group is then divided into two of equal size. The two group halves are now asked to stand in a line opposite to and facing each other in a large room. The following instructions are then given by the person running the exercise:

1. The person directly opposite for the purpose of this exercise is your partner.

2. Talking is not allowed during the exercise.

3. The task is to approach your partner, in what ever way you feel comfortable, bearing in mind what is writen on your card, and to get together with your partner either sitting or standing in order that you may begin a very serious conversation.

4. Once in the position they feel most comfortable with, the partners freeze.

The exercise then starts with the person running the exercise requesting the two lines to mill about for a moment or two before giving the instruction: '*Now will you please get together in order to carry out the task*'.

The exercise produces a lot of open hand movements, some dancing around as partners weigh each other up, partners who remain at a distance and others who get very close. Some will draw up chairs and sit, others will stand openly confronting, some pointing and using other gestures and even partners who turn back to back.

If it is possible to video the exercise participants will then be able to view their movements. If this is not possible the person running the exercise draws out the different forms of non-verbal communication signs by going round the group (making use of the non-verbal signs list), examining the various positions each of the couplets have adopted in relation to the information they were initially given about their partner. As each of the couplets are considered the persons under consideration are requested to read out what is written upon their card.

This simple exercise helps to identify the messages you give with your body. The learning points include:
- exploring of the process of mirroring which takes place when one partner may feel more insecure or threatened. Any mirroring which occurs is usually reacted to with surprise by those involved

- nervous smiles exhibited by most of the group, a common reaction to uncomfortable situations and a point to remain aware of whenever you face any uncomfortable situation such as aggression – a smile may be easily mistaken for a smirk
- the fact that each participant went into this 'interview' with their own agenda (information about their partner) which may have influenced their behaviour
- the effects of gestures upon partners
- the acknowledgement that non-verbal signs are open to interpretation and, although needing to be aware of these signs, you must remain equally aware that they are also open to misinterpretation
- identifying that culture, gender and other elements affect the messages given and received
- the amount of non-verbal information you give and receive
- the 'feelings' experienced
- helping to understand the way you are perceived by others
- helping to identify unhelpful body mannerisms which you may wish to amend.

Non-verbal signs are important to consider in any interaction and can be used as possible indicators of the build-up of aggression. The non-verbal signs to be aware of are:
- **physical closeness**
- **positioning**
- **physical contact**
- **posture**
- **facial expressions**
- **eye movement**
- **gestures**
- **head movement**
- **mirroring**
- **appearance.**

As about 70% of the communication which takes place between humans is non-verbal, in a potentially threatening situation it is important that you include body language in your assessment of individuals. At least then, if you recognize any of the factors which may indicate violence or aggression, you are prepared to act, if required.

The following are a number of points about the different signals. The information provided is by no means a comprehensive statement of each of these signals and if further information is required there are a number of books available which will give a more complete picture. Within the following explanations, some information is included concerning different cultural elements as, within a multi-ethnic society, moods and behaviours expressed by people with different cultural backgrounds, or different societal 'norms', need to be understood and interpreted outside an ethnocentric approach.

Physical closeness

Within English culture, it is accepted that you have a defendable space surrounding you. This space is effectively a semi-circle to the front and side of you which extends from the shoulder to the tips of your fingers held horizontally. If someone, whom you are not close to, enters this space you will feel uncomfortable, perhaps invaded and you are likely to react to this. You may become tense as muscles contract and inadvertently give a body message which may escalate the situation. You may show your fear, so adopting the victim role and implying to the aggressor consent to being treated as such. You may react purposefully or aggressively thereby verbally or non-verbally escalating the situation.

Exercise

1. Examine your interviewing facilities. Are the people you interview likely to feel that their defendable space is being encroached or invaded?

2. How might they react to this?

The defendable space at your back is situational and varies with circumstances. Imagine, for example, you are walking alone over an isolated moorland. It is getting dark and you hear a twig snap, somewhere in the distance behind you. Would you feel comfortable? Your defendable space here therefore, might be a 100 metres or more. Yet, if you were walking along a crowded street with people occasionally bumping into you as they pushed past, you would not necessarily feel discomfort. The feeling of discomfort generated when you are approached from behind therefore depends upon the circumstances in which you find yourself. This idea is important to consider when you are to interview anyone within your offices. Many of the people you see will be feeling uncomfortable and 'on edge' simply by being within what to them may be a strange and, in many instances, a formidable place i.e. your office. Imagine the reaction if you were to approach a visitor to your offices, who may well have come to discuss a highly charged emotional situation, from behind, or if you further increased their discomfort by encroaching into their personal space.

Different cultures have different perspectives on personal space. People from some cultures will, for example, feel extremely comfortable at being physically very close and may even edge up to you as you move away.

Exercise

1. Meet with colleagues from different ethnic backgrounds and discuss the concept of personal space with them.

2. Identify the personal space preferred by people from Spain/Germany/France/ Japan/England/West Indies.

Positioning

If someone stands face on to you they might be considered to be 'facing up' to you. Similarly, although you may both be seated, should the other person sit in such a way that they are directly in front of you, they block your exit and give you the message to be on your guard. You are now being given a 'face to face confrontation' message. If however, the other person moves their chair, placing it at an angle of about 90 degrees, so that your knees are close together and you are more or less side by side, you would not be blocked in. You now have the opportunity of walking away without walking through the other person. You are no longer in a confrontation situation. You are in effect receiving a signal that they are 'on your side'.

The way you stand is important too, not only because of the message which this may give to the person before you but also in relation to the 'target' area you may be offering to the aggressor. 'Front' on offers the aggressor the whole torso to strike at – a large area. However, if you stand at a slight angle, slightly turning your shoulder towards the aggressor, the surface area shown to the aggressor becomes smaller. Besides signalling non-aggression standing at a slight angle offers the aggressor less of a target and increases the chances of receiving a glancing blow as opposed to a full on blow.

Positioning becomes important when considering your approach to someone who may be signalling aggression. Should you walk towards them straight on – which may be interpreted as threatening, or do you attempt to approach the person from a slight angle? Do you stride purposefully towards them or stroll casually? These questions must be given due consideration before the situation occurs.

Exercise

1. Decide how you would approach the following:
- A drunken middle-aged man threatening a fellow worker
- A distraught mother who believes you have harmed her child
- A disruptive group of teenagers intimidating a younger child

2. With a colleague discuss your answers and consider the possible outcomes of your approaches.

Physical contact

In English culture it is unusual to witness a great deal of physical contact outside close relationships. Perhaps the greatest amount of physical contact involves the ritualistic hand-shaking which occurs at meetings and partings. You need be aware of this, particularly if, when faced with aggression, you feel inclined to touch the aggressor, a gesture which you perceive as calming, showing concern or as containing. As physical contact is rare the aggressor may perceive this action as a double escalation and an affront. First, you have entered their defendable space and then you have initiated contact. By making physical contact you have signalled to the aggressor that they may touch you in return, and that return touch may be a slap, a push away or some other form of contact higher up the scale. Alternatively, should the aggressor make physical contact, maybe in the form of prodding with a finger, you need to be aware that the scale has been raised and you need to take action to address this before there is a further escalation.

If you need to consider making physical contact, the offer of an open hand, in the acknowledged and acceptable form of a handshake, may be an acceptable method of attempting to defuse the aggression. However, not everyone employs or is aware of the social etiquette of a handshake and it therefore becomes necessary to consider the cultural norms which may affect the perceptions of the person concerned.

Some cultures engage in, and react to, physical contact differently. Think about people from Spain, Germany, France and Poland – what might be the rules governing the use of physical contact within these societies? What are your experiences in meeting people from these backgrounds?

Exercise

1. Note down any forms of physical contact between yourself and a person from Spain, Germany, France or Poland. Consider in particular the use of handshakes, kisses and hugs.

2. Discuss your answers with a colleague.

In some eastern countries the accepted western norm of formal greeting, the handshake, has been adopted and is employed in particular when east meets west. Japanese businessmen may no longer bow in formal greeting yet this remains their culturally accepted form of greeting. The salutation where the hands are placed together, palms touching with fingers pointing upwards, in front of the chest accompanied with a slight bow may not be commonplace in certain parts of English society yet this remains a culturally accepted norm for many people with an Asian background. Certain religions require that physical contact does not take place between certain sections of society, or at certain times. For example, some cultures will not allow physical contact with a woman who is menstruating.

It is important not necessarily to be aware of all the different cultural elements but to remain aware of the everyday assumptions you make when applying your own cultural norms to people you meet. For example, will you automatically offer your hand in greeting without first considering the culture of the person before you?

Exercise

1. What are the cultural norms which you adopt/take for granted when meeting or being introduced to a stranger for the first time?

2. Do the rules governing physical contact vary according to the situation i.e. formal/informal/social/office-based etc?

Posture

Posture can indicate mood. It can show whether you feel secure or threatened, happy or sad, pleased or annoyed. The statue of 'The Thinker' shows a person in an actively thoughtful mood. This can be seen even from a distance simply because of the pose the model has assumed. He is not annoyed, not angry and not sad – he is deep in thought.

Consider his posture. Now consider the posture of a person who is very sad. Their shoulders may be slouched, head hung down, muscles relaxed and their arms may be hanging limp at their sides. Finally, consider the body posture of an aggressive person. What are the body signals? Their shoulders may be more square and hunched upwards as the muscles around the neck are tightened, they could point either towards or away from the victim. Their upper torso will be tense with fists possibly clenched, or their hands may be opening and closing as they wind themselves up. Their arms could be held purposefully slightly away from the sides with a small, yet noticeable, slight bend at the elbow.

Exercise

1. List the posture features of a relaxed person.

2. List the opposite to these features.

Posture is also influenced by cultural background. An Asian man may be required to demonstrate deference to an elder, a person in authority or a married woman and does this by adopting a submissive posture.

White, male terminology influences thinking with such phrases as 'an honest, upstanding sort' and 'as straight as a die' which leads western minds to believe that slouching is a sign of a weak character while square shoulders indicate strength of character.

Exercise

1. Identify other phrases which are culturally based and may influence your perceptions.

In any meeting with an aggressor you should remain aware of your body posture. It is difficult not to want to adopt a counter position to that being shown by the aggressor (mirror image). Your natural reaction is to want to meet force with force. However, if you can maintain a calm, relaxed posture:
- you do not escalate the situation
- you signal to the aggressor that you remain in control, and
- you give the aggressor the opportunity to mirror your calmness.

Facial expressions

You know when someone is happy. They smile, their face 'lights up', there is a relaxation of muscles about the eyes and the forehead, the pupils of the eyes dilate and the eyebrows may be slightly raised.

Similarly you are given indications when someone is becoming aggressive. Their mouth may be tightened, teeth clenched or lower jaw held tightly set, the corners of the mouth tend to angle downwards, there may be a deepening of the furrows above the bridge of the nose, eyebrows may be pulled together as the muscles around the face tighten, the openings of the nostril may widen and contract rhythmically as they breathe through mouth and nose more rapidly. At the side of the forehead a nervous tic may be seen pulsing through a vein, another may pulse through a vein in the neck just below the jaw bone, as the blood is pumped rapidly from the heart. Pupils may become smaller, and muscles beneath the eyes may contract pulling the lids slightly together narrowing the amount of eye shown and increasing the impression that the aggressor is staring.

All these are indicators to be considered. However, remember that everyone can be sophisticated in the use of facial expressions and in hiding their true intent behind a facial mask. Therefore in some instances it will not be the overt signs which will show themselves, but the more subtle changes in the facial expression, for example, a frozen, detached smile or minor indications of a tightening around the mouth and/or eyes, or an increase in the rate of breathing giving rise to slightly flaring nostrils.

Remember too that in other cultures facial expressions may not mean the same or portray the same as within a western culture. In Japan, for example, it is expected that irrespective of how you feel you will retain a smile.

Exercise

1. Together with a partner practise facial expressions. Try happy/sad/angry/ hostile/irritated etc.

2. Identify the subtle, and not so subtle, indications which make up these expressions.

Eye movement

The use of the eyes as a communication device is influenced by culture. In some cultures it is considered impolite for a woman to look directly into the eyes of a man, or, for a boy to look into the eyes of his elders. Other cultures insist that young people, irrespective of their age, must show deference by keeping their eyes down when speaking to an elder. Some cultures however, suggest that if you wish to be considered to be honest, forthright and trustworthy then eye contact is imperative.

In an incident of escalating aggression the aggressor may stare purposefully at the victim, alternatively s/he may fail to make eye contact altogether. Should the former occur then it becomes the responsibility of the potential victim to break off eye contact as a way of attempting to de-escalate the situation. It is not suggested that you need to turn away, or to take your attention away from the aggressor, because this could give the aggressor the opportunity to strike. It is important to consider how you break off the stare, for example, by looking down at the aggressor's feet you might signal 'victim', and this could lead to a further escalation as the aggressor attempts to stress dominance.

You can break a stare simply by moving your focus from the aggressor's eyes, to their forehead, along the forehead, down to the mouth and then back again to the eyes or forehead. Breaking a stare is not easy as the need to continue with the challenge can remain very strong within you.

Should the aggressor choose not to establish eye contact, it becomes the responsibility of the potential victim to maintain a watchful vigilance while paradoxically attempting to establish eye contact without staring. Keeping the head up and eyes, without staring focused on the aggressor's head, indicates a willingness to establish eye contact and will be open to any furtive glances the aggressor may throw.

Exercise

1. Consider the occasions when you have been engaged in a staring match. What were your feelings at the time?

Gestures

Gestures communicate ideas, feelings and instructions. A casual wave of an open hand may indicate one thing while a clenched fist thrust suddenly to within inches of the face will suggest another. A pointed finger usually implies an instruction or command, a raised thumb suggests good news while raised middle fingers jerked upwards express a derogatory message. Gestures can be difficult to deal with as they can evoke retaliatory reactions within yourself. Gestures, like all forms of non-verbal signals, can be misinterpreted particularly by someone in an emotional state. Therefore it is necessary to examine the everyday gestures you make use of and to consider modifying any which may be open to misinterpretation.

Pointing at the person with whom you are communicating, or jabbing the air with a finger as a way of stressing a point are both gestures which may be considered to be escalatory. Using a pen as an extention of a finger to point can be viewed in the same way, and knocking a desk with the knuckles of a clenched fist can bring the attention required but can also be perceived as anger or hostility to an observer and be responded to as such. Tapping or strumming the desk with a finger may be interpreted as irritability when in fact you are silently humming your favourite tune.

Exercise

1. Identify any everyday gestures you have which may be open to misinterpretation when dealing with an aggressive person. If you are unable to identify any for yourself talk to a colleague or friend and ask them to point any out for you.

Generally, open hand language, with slow, purposeful movements is a method of expressing calmness and control while closed hand messages indicates the reverse.

The use and expression of gestures can be different according to culture and whilst florid arms movements are more common in people from one culture, more conservative arm and body movements may be more common in another.

When dealing with an aggressive person use the following as a rough guideline in relation to your gestures:
- keep your movements slow and fluid
- use open hand communication
- do not point
- keep your gestures to a minimum
- nod occasionally to show you are listening
- keep your hands as visible as possible.

Exercise

1. What gestures do people from the different cultural backgrounds listed use to express the following emotions:

	Happiness	Anger	Excitement
West Indies			
Germany			
India			
Japan			
Ireland			
England			

Exercise

Consider the following scenario and answer the questions.
You walk into a crowded and noisy waiting area and are immediately and unexpectedly confronted by a large, angry man. His shoulders are hunched up, and with his fingers closed together almost forming a fist, he is jabbing the air just before you, his pointing finger barely stopping short of your chest. He demands to see you alone.

1. How would you feel?

2. What would be your first action, and why?

3. How will you signal non-aggression?

4. What should you be watching for?

5. What are the signs which signal escalation?

Head movements

A head nod can be a reinforcer used to encourage more communication, or a method of attempting to speed up the interaction.

If you want someone to know that you are listening, you will indicate it with an occasional, perhaps almost indiscernible nod. If your head nods become intermittently frequent and exaggerated while the other person is talking, you are perhaps becoming more involved. If, on the other hand, there is no intermission between the exaggerated nods the message you are giving has changed. You might be wanting them to 'get on with it' or you might want to get away. You are certainly no longer showing an interest in them.

Head nods which are not synchronized with the speaker are important to watch for as they indicate that the listener is not necessarily engaged in the content and/or process of the communication.

In addition to head nods, head shakes may be another indication of disengaging from communication. It is virtually impossible to get a message across to anyone who is repeatedly shaking their head violently. If this activity is accompanied by the repetition of a word or phrase then the person who is attempting to communicate needs to be aware that the other person concerned is creating a barrier through which it is highly unlikely that any information will pass. If you are confronted with this sort of behaviour think very carefully about your need to remain where you are. If at all possible leave.

Mirroring

Mirroring can take place when two or more individuals meet. Without realizing it, you can adopt the positions and mannerisms of the person before you. This reflection of image is done as a way of either subconsciously attempting to put the person opposite you at their ease, or as a way of putting yourself at ease.

Mirroring is usually a subconscious reaction. It is often done at time of stress or discomfort and can be easily seen in an interview situation. It may a complementary gesture; and is used by some as a tool – which can be as powerful as the reflective form of counselling used by many counsellors. The active or passive use of mirroring is necessary to consider in aggressive situations because by assuming the postures, mannerisms and gestures of the aggressor, you can unwittingly escalate the situation or by encouraging the aggressor to adopt your own smoothing and calming mannerisms you can help defuse the situation.

Exercise

1. Sit opposite a colleague or friend and mirror their mannerisms.

2. Ask them to mirror yours.

3. Discuss what feelings different gestures evoke.

Appearance

First impressions count and can influence the way you perceive and react to a person or a place. In turn, your perceptions and your reactions could be picked up and acted upon by the person concerned, and so you can establish a reactive cycle which can inhibit productive communication.

Exercise

1. What are the important visual cues you look for when you meet someone for the first time?

Factors for a good image	Factors for a poor image
1.	1.
2.	2.
3.	3.
4.	4.
5.	5.
6.	6.
7.	7.

2. What do the cues/factors say to you about the person concerned?

1.	1.
2.	2.
3.	3.
4.	4.
5.	5.
6.	6.
7.	7.

3. Why?

1.	1.
2.	2.
3.	3.
4.	4.
5.	5.
6.	6.
7.	7.

Appearance can highlight a deterioration in a persons' ability or desire to care for themselves and you should be aware of this if you see the person relatively frequently. In an aggressive situation, if the aggressor has lost the desire to care for him/herself, then you should be thinking 'If they don't care for themselves then how can I expect them to show any care/any concern for me?'

It is also important that you remain aware of your own appearance even if it is just to ensure that you do not offer the aggressor a weapon or means of damaging you. Large, dangling earrings are easily pulled; long hair which falls in front of you should you duck to miss a blow could be grabbed allowing your face to be slammed into a desk; in glasses, plastic lenses cost no more than glass ones but do not smash or cut you if you are hit in the face; low heeled shoes allow you to run better than high ones; a tie grabbed and held stops you from leaving; a tight skirt or dress will not allow you the freedom to run.

Exercise

1. Identify those items which you wear that could be used against you.

2. Consider what message your reception area and interviewing facilities give to the people using them.

3. Identify any different cultural features which you are aware of, and which may be misinterpreted, by persons from different cultures as aggression.

7

Verbal Indications

Equally important are the verbal signals which may precede a violent or aggressive event – which are all too often missed, ignored or simply not taken seriously. The verbal signals to consider include:
- threats either to the organization or to the individual
- depersonalizing language
- repetitive language
- emotional content/tone of speech.

Threats

Threats should be taken seriously and a strategy employed, or at least considered, to deal with them. Often, however, the threat is not directed towards the individual but towards the agency concerned.

How many receptionists and switchboard personnel hear such threats as: *'You send someone round and there'll be trouble'* or *'If I have to come in to that office there's gonna be a problem'*, but do not report it?.

A verbal threat is a clear message. If you fail to act upon the messages given to you then you can further frustrate the speaker and the message may take a different form. That different form may be a more severe threat, verbal abuse or even physical contact. The threat may have been uttered in the heat of the moment, as a way of commanding attention, as a one-off expression of anger or it may be the preliminary to an assault. Irrespective of the reason for it, if you fail to act upon the information given, you fail in your task to reduce the potential for violence.

Verbal threats should always be treated seriously as they indicate a potential for physical violence.

Exercise

1. How does your agency deal with threats against staff?

2. How do you deal with threats?

Depersonalizing language

Depersonalizing language can take two forms:
1. It can be used by an aggressor to depersonalize the individual. In this form the aggressor is able to merge the individual into a heterogeneous group. This identification allows the aggressor to strike out at anonymous body and deny that an individual stands before them. This form of depersonalizing language may be recognized by the use of such phrases as: *'you lot'* and *'you're all the same'*. Or it may be expressed in the form of dehumanizing individuals with words such as: 'slut, slag, bastards etc'.

   Depersonalizing language often occurs in racial attacks. For the aggressor, it removes the emphasis from damaging individual human beings and allows them to damage the object concerned, in this case 'Blacks' or 'Chinks' etc. The aggressor may damage an 'object', as represented by the individual present, without immediate loss of self-esteem, sometimes such actions even increase personal and group status.
2. It can be used by the aggressor to depersonalize themselves. Here the aggressor replaces first person singular usage (I) with second person singular usage (you) or the plural (we) each time using the noun or pronoun to refer to self. For example, *'We could take you'*, when the aggressor is referring to self, or *'You could really hurt this one'*, again where the aggressor is alone and referring to self.

   Be aware that where a potential aggressor is making use of language to depersonalize him/ herself, or to depersonalize you, this should be considered a device used to wind up for an act of violence. Be on your guard.

Repetitive language

A spontaneous act of violence is not easy to initiate. Generally, the situation needs to build up to an overt expression of violence and one way of achieving this is to repetitively verbalize this build up. In individuals, this verbal repetition, changing emphasis, stressing certain words or phrases and increasing in tempo and pitch becomes an indicator for a potential act of violence.

'I'm gonna get you. I mean it. I do. I'll get you. I will. I'll get you!' Do not ignore the threat. Listen to the content and address it positively. Make use of the defusing techniques outlined on pages 85–91.

Within groups this repetitive build up can be identified as a ritualistic chant. In some cultures and groups it is used as a method of encouraging aggression. For example, when groups of supporters engage in chanting as a method of encouraging their team or as a way of intimidating an opposing set of supporters.

Exercise

It is early Saturday afternoon. You are walking alone down the street when, from around a corner, a group of youths suddenly appear. They are repetitively chanting, *'We are the greatest'*. In the background you hear the sound of bottles being smashed. The group is about 50 metres from you and is walking purposefully towards you. At least one member of the group has seen you and is signalling this to the others. Except for you and the youths the street is deserted.

1. What would you need to be aware of in these circumstances and why?

2. What would you do in this situation and why?

Emotional content/tone of speech

Within individual situations, it is important not only to be aware of what is being said but also to be aware of the manner and tone in which it is being spoken. The words 'I'm fine' spoken through clenched teeth, with the emphasis on either or both words, might indicate anger or agitation, while the same phrase spoken in a relaxed manner, maybe with a reinforcing gentle nod of the head and a casual, warm smile indicates something completely different.

However, you cannot automatically assume that tone, emphasis or emotional content is a firm indicator of the situation particularly when you are dealing with people from a different culture. Different ethnic groups can place a different emphasis on syllables and words to that expected by the listener. This unexpected emphasis can be interpreted by a person from a different culture as abrupt or rude, whereas a person from the same culture would find the tone and statement courteous and polite. This difference in expression and tone can easily be misunderstood and lead to an abrupt and inappropriate response on behalf of the listener, which, in turn could be perceived as aggressive.

In some cases, this misunderstanding in communication can inadvertently form the roots of racial hostility. For example, have you ever been in a newsagent managed by an Asian and walked away with the impression that the shopkeeper was rude, perhaps because of the abrupt manner in which s/he expressed her/himself? Have your feelings ever been bruised by the manner in which a person not from your cultural background expressed themselves? Do you maintain the stereotypical perception that Americans are pushy simply because they are louder or express themselves more forcibly than you do?

The tone expressed by the subject of the aggression is equally important when it comes to helping to defuse the situation. By keeping your tone calm and your voice quiet you do not encourage the aggressor to increase their level or pitch. In fact, you actively discourage both as, in order to listen to what you have to say, the aggressor is forced to become quieter. Furthermore, by maintaining a calming and soothing tone in your voice you are signalling to the aggressor:

- non-escalation
- non-aggression, and
- that you remain in control.

Incongruity

Watch for incongruity, when perhaps words and actions are not syncronized, as a potential indicator that something is wrong. Once spotted address the incongruity.

Signs and signals summary

- First impressions do count.
- Be alert to the possibility of violence.
- Listen for what is being said *and* the way it is being said.
- Be aware of your own body messages.
- Be aware of the other persons' body messages.

- Watch out for escalation.
- Deal with aggression at an early stage.
- Take threats seriously.
- Keep your movements slow.
- Keep your tone calm and reassuring.
- Use open hand language.
- Allow the aggressor space.
- Stay calm.
- Be aware of cultural differences in speech and tone.

8

Additional and Incidental Factors

Exercise

1. Consider the circumstances concerning any act of violence or aggression in which you or someone close to you has been involved. Make a list of the factors under two separate headings:

   Information/factors known   Information/factors gained
   before the incident   following the incident

Case study 2

This incident was particularly unpleasant. It involved a client with a known history of mental ill health, although at the time of the incident she was not considered, by the worker whose assessment ability had always been sound, to be unwell.

The agency involved had, on occasion, provided finance to various families to purchase food, as a method of ensuring the children in those families remained out of care. The client concerned had witnessed this process when a few weeks previously an aggressive father had demanded, and was given, some money for food for his children.

Mary, a woman in her early 30s had no children and lived alone. She had spent what little money she had the previous day and was now without food or small change for the gas meter, her only form of heating. She had tried begging on the street earlier in the day but gave this up and became distressed when she was sexually harrassed.

Initially she had telephoned the office in tears only to be told that her worker was not available. It was then that she became abusive and began to demand money. She became even more abusive when the telephonist tried to reason with her and she threatened to call into the office to get some money. She also threatened to 'get' the worker if the money was not available because, *'he never does anything for me anyway.'* This conversation was not passed on to the worker concerned as the receptionist who took the call put it down to 'normal-type' behaviour for Mary.

It was well known within the office that the receptionist frequently made such assessments. *'If we get told every time someone threatens us we'll never leave the office'* a worker said later in defence of the action.

Later that morning Mary stormed into the reception area and banged at the glass reception panel ranting that she wanted her rights, just like everyone else! The worker, who was very skilled, experienced and caring in dealing with clients, was called out of a case conference to deal with her. He went downstairs to interview Mary feeling furious that the duty worker had not been called to at least try to calm her down in the first instance. The first thing he said to her was, *'Look Mary, I don't have time for this.'* She shouted back that she wanted her rights. She was just like everyone else and she wanted to be treated like a normal person. He insisted that he had always treated her as normal and that was why he was now saying that he was going back to his meeting and he would see her later! With that he turned and left.

As the worker returned upstairs, Mary became more irritated and shouted threateningly after him that she would 'get him'. Some moments later Mary followed him upstairs and then stalked menacingly along the corridor outside the different offices, banging doors and shouting, *'I'm waiting'* and *'I want to be treated like everyone else'* and *'I'll show you'*. Her shouting was interspersed with derogatory comments, repetitive mumbling and swear words.

The worker reappeared in an attempt to 'calm her'. He was still not aware of the reason for her initial distress and told her she would have to wait downstairs. She refused and an argument developed which quickly reached shouting level. The argument continued at shouting pitch for some moments and eventually when in the midst of it all Mary shouted that she needed some money the worker's immediate response was, *'No way Mary. We're not a charity'.*

Mary swung her handbag at him hitting him in the head. She then pushed him against a wall where she held him for some minutes, all the time shouting and screaming into his face, threatening his life. The threats and shouting continued almost unabated with the worker pushed up against the wall. The worker was shocked and had frozen and remained in this position, for what seemed an inordinate period of time before the police appeared and pulled Mary away from him.

1. Consider case study 2 and identify the elements which contributed to the violence and/ or those which indicated that violence was a possibility.

From Case Study 2 a number of points emerge which come under the heading of predictive factors for indicating the potential for violence. Before considering these, however, other equally important issues followed the incident and it became clear that these issues had a direct influence on the event. These issues must be considered as additional factors.

Some weeks later at a meeting to discuss the incident a number of factors were identified:

1. The only manager around at the time of the incident had been newly appointed from a basic grade post. It was, however, fortunate that a manager was available at all. The practice in the office had, until this incident, been to leave the office without a manager other than at the end of a telephone. The manager had been the one who telephoned the police, because no-one else in the office felt they had the authority to do so.

2. The manager concerned had not known at which point to intercede, feeling that by doing so prematurely the worker would be undermined in front of his client and colleagues. Yet, by leaving the situation to develop the worker was the subject of an attack.

3. Other staff in the office also shared the same feeling as the manager; and had not wished to be viewed as 'interfering' between client and worker. Others, understandably, admitted to being afraid to intervene and expressed a feeling of relief that this was not their client and that this was not happening to them.

4. Both manager and staff were now experiencing feelings of guilt for not intervening.

5. No policy existed concerning interviewing potentially violent clients.

6. No policy existed regarding the involvement of the police.

7. Within the office different staff members had different views of what was considered to be 'acceptable' and 'unacceptable' client behaviour. Some expressed the view that clients ranted and raved frequently. They were not alerted therefore to the potential danger in this situation as this level of client behaviour was within the bounds of normality for their workplace.

8. All offices were accessible from the reception area by staff *and* clients. Once inside the reception area, no part of the building was secure.

9. Although the agency concerned did have an overall policy on violence towards staff the operation of this policy was left to individual workers and was open to individual interpretation. For example, no standard pattern was established regarding the provision of support to an individual who was subjected to an incident. In effect, this meant that the 'victim' was left to decide whether or not to prosecute the aggressor; whether or not to remain at work or take sick leave and whether or not they should request counselling.

10. The worker had wanted *anyone* in the office to show themselves and felt abandoned by colleagues and managers who failed to appear while the incident was taking place.

11. The worker had received no formal training in defusing violence and had no knowledge about the possible effects of violence. He had 'frozen', was unable to shout for assistance and now because of this felt totally deskilled.

12. The worker had been off sick since the incident and felt even more unsupported and let down by colleagues and managers because they had failed to telephone him to ask how he was.

Exercise

1. What can be done in the future to minimize the possibility of a similar event occurring within this office?

2. Have you, or one of your colleagues, ever experienced a similar violent situation?

What were the circumstances?

What has been done to reduce the chance of a similar event occurring again?

What is still outstanding?

9

Predictive Factors

History

Has the aggressor concerned previously been abusive and/or aggressive towards other individuals? This includes other workers. Although not mentioned in case study 2 Mary did have a history of aggressive behaviour. However, it was considered by those presently working on the case that, as these episodes occurred two, or even three years earlier, that this behaviour was obsolete (there was no clear indication of these occurrances recorded on the present file being used).

Where there is a history of violent behaviour it must be considered as it provides evidence that the client is capable of such behaviour and any assessment must take this into consideration.

If you are considering previous history be aware of:
- the precise form of aggressive behaviour shown
- the factors which led up to the expression of violence
- what caused the behaviour
- the severity of the behaviour
- how it was handled, and
- what the outcomes were.

Also remember that your records will be the history in future and it is both useful, and indeed good practice, to record occurrences of violent behaviour using the above format.

Behaviour

1. **Does an assessment of the current behaviour presented by the client indicate unpredictability in actions and/or responses?**
   Unpredictable behaviour is difficult to deal with. Plan a strategy, do not see the person alone and let colleagues know where you are.
2. **Is the behaviour escalating?**
   Mary's behaviour (in case study 2) leading up to the incident was escalatory. Firstly, she telephoned the office and made demands and threats. Secondly, she arrived at the office angry and demanding. Thirdly, she threatened the worker when she saw him. Then she followed the worker upstairs and walked up and down the corridor demanding attention, and finally she carried out her threatened action. At no stage was she told that this behaviour was unacceptable.

   Remain alert to the behaviour of the potential aggressor. Watch out for escalation:
   - rhythmic movement (body rocking/tapping/continous head nods/foot stamping etc)
   - tense muscles (around the mouth, clenched teeth, neck and shoulders, hands, clenched fist etc)
   - escalatory mannerisms (pointing or jabbing a finger or object, staring, increasing tempo or

tone in speech, encroachment into personal space, sudden movements, depersonalized language etc).

Threats

From the initial contact in case study 2 and up until the violent incident, Mary had made various threats which were either ignored, considered as part of her pathology or not addressed.

Threats must be taken seriously and a strategy devised so that they can be addressed, with the person making the threat, in an environment which offers protection to the victim. Always remember, it need not be left up to the subject of the threat to address it, although s/he may wish to and should be offered the opportunity within a strategy meeting.

Threats can come in two different forms:

1. Threats to the organization, *'You send someone round here and see what happens'*, *'you lot need something doing to make you sit up'*, *'if I don't get my money there'll be trouble'*.

   How many times do clients telephone and leave such messages which do not get passed on simply because it is put down to their normal behaviour pattern: *'Well, that's David. He's always saying things like that.'*

2. Threats to the individual, *'I'll sort you out'*, *'I'm gonna get you'*, *'you come round here and you know what to expect'*.

Exercise

1. What are the possible consequences of failing to address the threat: *'I'm gonna get you'*.

2. Work out a strategy for addressing such a threat from a person with whom you are involved.

Appearance

In case study 2, Mary arrived in the reception area looking dishevelled and unkempt. This initial appearance was put down to the fact that she had probably rushed to the office. However, this may not have been the case – Mary's appearance as a potential indicator of her personal esteem was not considered.

It is important to consider the manner (not type) and standard of dress and hygiene presented. This may not be easy particularly if the person is not known to the agency beforehand. It becomes easier when a more comprehensive assessment of the person's failure to care for themselves can be completed in a situation where the person is known to the worker or agency.

Failure to maintain personal standards could indicate a lowering of self-esteem. The question then arises that if the aggressor has poor self-esteem what esteem will s/he have for others? It is easier for a person with low self-esteem to be violent than a person with high self-esteem.

Possessions

Holding, touching or taking someone's possessions must be viewed as a potential flash point for the expression of anger. With any form of interactive contact the removal of any possession (e.g. taking a child into care), the denial of a possession (e.g. procedures to be followed before money is given) or physical contact with a client's possession (e.g. turning a television set down or dragging a dog out of a room to reduce the noise or distraction level) must be considered as potential escalation points. Where the removal of a client's possessions is to take place strategies for the prevention or minimalization of violence must be considered.

Removal of liberty

The removal of liberty is a potentially dangerous situation. To deprive anyone of what they perceive as their basic rights will create a situation of anger and hostility and must be very carefully handled.

Irrespective of the circumstances, if the removal or restriction of a person's liberty is to be undertaken, strategies for the prevention or minimalization of violence must be considered. This consideration must also take into account the potential reactions of the person's family in particular children, siblings and partner.

Environment

Environment can be important to consider when dealing with a potentially violent person. In case study 2 the violent incident took place within an office; there were other staff around and the surroundings were familiar to the victim, who felt reasonably secure.

It is important that staff feel secure within their workplace. However, this feeling of security can lead to a blasé attitude when dealing with aggressive clients, particularly where the client is already known to the worker. This must be guarded against.

In case study 2 the worker failed to read, or act upon, the signs being clearly given by his client. He was rushed and also, as he later put it, he did not think he could be violated 'on his own turf'. Ensuring staff security is important for all employers and even more so when employees are called upon to deal with potentially violent people. A number of simple precautions could help increase the security of workers in most workplaces.

- Locked doors with security-coded buttons.
- Panic buttons in interview rooms or located strategically throughout a building will enable assistance to be summoned.
- Personal alarms carried by staff, perhaps worn on a belt, could achieve similar results.
- A security guard may have a mollifying influence on behaviour.
- Adequate lighting within buildings will increase the feeling of security particularly in reception areas or along corridors.
- A well lit, airy reception, office or workplace will engender a feeling of worth in both the worker and the client.
- Lighting around a building, particularly in car park areas or around the front porch, will help with getting the key into the lock on a dark, wintery evening.
- Adequate lighting and the provision of a few simple inexpensive devices increases the feeling of personal security and will help reduce the potential for violence occurring.

Check-list for working outside the station

The above are a few ideas which could help increase the security of a workplace. However, if a lot of your work is done outside of a work station, as much thought as possible must be given to the environment in which you are to venture. Consider the following as a check-list:

- Will it be light or dark when I arrive?
- Are the streets lit?
- Will I be walking along any deserted areas?
- Am I visiting a block of flats?
- Do the lifts work?
- Are there any walkways to walk through?
- Will there be any other people around?
- Is it a run down estate/area?
- Where is the nearest shop/place to escape to?
- Will the shop/safe place be open at the time of my visit?
- Is there much activity in the area?
- Do I feel safe? Why/why not?
- Am I carrying a personal alarm?
- Do I know the occupant(s) of the premises?
- Am I visiting alone?
- Have I left notification of my movements back at the office?
- If I am doing a late visit do I have a reporting back system?

(*see* also the section on Home Visits, page 75)

Alcohol and drugs

Alcohol and/or drugs can remove inhibitions and alter a person's perceptions of social convention. In case study 2, it was later discovered that Mary had ceased taking medication, against medical advice, for several days. This may have been a contributory factor. Had the worker been aware of this information, no doubt his initial assessment of the situation, and his opening contact with Mary, would have been influenced by this.

Whereas, it may be difficult to identify whether or not a person is under the influence of drugs, or, in fact withdrawing from them, it is slightly easier to determine if a person has been drinking. However, not many agencies have a policy concerning contact with an intoxicated person.

Solvents are another problem which can affect an individual's functioning and reasoning ability. Irrespective of the length of time you may have known the person and the belief that you have a 'good relationship' with them, any person under the influence of solvents must be considered a high risk when it comes to the potential to inflict violence.

Exercise

1. What is your agency's staff policy for dealing with people under the influence of alcohol/solvents.

Weapons

It may be self-evident to state that the availability of a weapon is a contributory factor to the possibility of violence taking place. However, as well as weapons carried by the individual themselves, such as knives, belts, chains etc., there are many other incidental weapons which you might inadvertently provide.

Look around your place of work and make a list of the variety of projectiles and heavy, moveable objects which can be, and often are, used as weapons. Glass or metal ashtrays, tubular chairs, wooden chairs, telephones, letter openers, wooden play blocks and other older heavier children's toys can all be used in assaults. Other weapons might include lighted cigarettes pressed on an exposed part of the body, hot drinks thrown particularly in the face, stiletto heels, hypodermic needles with the threat of injecting the Aids virus, items worn about the neck (ties/ chains) and earrings grabbed and pulled through pierced ears etc. Think of how you could minimize the availability of these potential weapons. Within residential and day care establishments knives and scissors put away in drawers may be all that can be done. However, make sure that even this simple precaution is taken, and consider too what other precautions for reducing the availability of weapons can be taken. Remember, it is not your responsibility to attempt to remove any weapon from a client. Call the police.

Attitude of the worker

The attitude of workers involved in violent situations is an important element to consider under the heading of predictive factors.

Many workers often feel that it is their responsibility to 'do something' because this is *their* client. Workers may either feel a responsibility for the client's behaviour or are concerned that their client's behaviour is in some way reflective of the worker's skills. A strong instinct may be to try to sort out the violent situation yourself. However, think before you rush in.

Within a residential establishment the strict adherence to rules and regulations by the worker can create difficulties at critical times such as meals, going to bed, getting up etc. Yet flexibility in many workers' eyes is viewed as a potential for anarchy. Residential work has always been difficult, and no more so than at present, when the theory of 'normalization', which expects residents to take as much control over their lives as possible, can so easily conflict with one or more of the existing rules of the establishment.

Exercise

1. Look at the rules and regulations which exist within your establishment.

2. List those rules which exist simply because 'they've always been there' and/or those which require alteration.

---

3. What can be done with each of these rules?

4. Which rules and regulations create conflict?

5. Are there any ways in which these rules can be changed in order to reduce the amount of conflict?

6. Where the answer is 'No', how can the possible conflict created be handled constructively?

7. Consider any case(s) of violence which have taken place in your work. What predictive factors are now apparent?

10

Home Visits

Case study 3

I visited the victim of attempted assault. The victim was not on the telephone so I was unable to discuss my visit prior to actually turning up. I had previously spoken to the detective in charge of the case who had mentioned drugs in connection with the state of the victim. There was very little other information about the victim, save brief details about the attempted assault. She had been walking through a local park at midday when a group of youths approached her. They threatened her and demanded she hand over her handbag and any money. She was grabbed from behind, but released almost immediately as a police car drove in the main gate. The youths ran away and were not apprehended. The victim was very shaken by the incident.

I decided to call on my way home, as I passed the road leading to the estate on my way to and from the office, and, as I was going on annual leave the following day, I decided to deal with this referral beforehand.

When I arrived at the address, it was getting dark. There were no lights on outside or inside that I could see. The streets around the maisonette were deserted. I had parked my car on the main road for security as the area had a reputation for vandalism.

The maisonette was up a flight of external steps to the first floor, the porch at the top being unlit. There was no sound from inside, and I noticed the front door glass was broken and patched with cardboard. It occurred to me that it may be a squat. I rang the bell, and getting no reply, knocked several times. The door was opened by a tall, young man who said nothing. He just stood there waiting. I asked for the woman by name, and said she was probably expecting me (or at least someone from my agency).

He said 'You'd better come in then', and stood back while I passed into the (unlit) hall. When he closed the front door, there was almost complete darkness. He directed me down the passage to a door on the left, at the end. In there I found the victim; and lights and the television on. I introduced myself, she introduced the young man as her boyfriend, and we all talked for about two hours. The couple, among other problems, had been or still were heroin addicts.

When I came away I realized that I had put myself into a potentially dangerous situation. The place had not been a squat, but by thinking it might have been, I should have been prepared for the door to be opened by anyone, not just someone relevant to my visit. Upon the door being opened, I should not have entered until I could see exactly where I was going (but is it rude to ask someone to turn a light on before you enter their home?). Having entered, I walked past the young man, into the gloom, and he closed the door behind us – a ridiculously vulnerable position to put myself into, and I had felt uncomfortable at the time.

Once in there, as it happens, everything was fine, and I was able to be of some use to the couple. However on reflection, I had not acknowledged the dangers, nor worked out an escape route for myself had things gone wrong.

1. Identify the factors which indicated the lack of safety for the worker in case study 3.

Preparation

Many workers visit clients outside the office environment, either calling at the home of the client or seeing the person in the community or in a community resource, e.g. a cafe, park, the home of the client's friend etc. Although everyday occurrences for many staff, all such visits require particular preparation and the possibility of violence taking place while on such a visit must be considered as a part of this preparation.

Preparation is particularly necessary when the visit is:
- to a person not previously known
- to a person with a known history of violence
- to remove a person's liberty
- to remove a possession
- to remove a child from the family
- to a person with unpredictable behaviour
- to give unwelcome information
- to a person under the influence of drugs, alcohol or solvents.

Exercise

1. List any additional factors important to your particular work situation.

Planning any contact is important even if it only takes the form of thinking about the initial approach on the way there. More comprehensive planning however will include:

- discussion with a colleague/supervisor beforehand
- listing 'risk' elements associated with this particular client/visit and identifying ways of minimizing these
- identifying the purpose of the visit and acknowledging to yourself that this purpose can be set aside if it is necessary to address and deal with aggressive behaviour, and
- running through the method(s) available to you to defuse aggressive behaviour.

Appropriate dress

- If you need to run, flat shoes are better than ones with heels.
- Ties can be grabbed, holding you where you are or pulling your head into an object. Tuck it into a shirt or wear an easily detachable one.
- Long, dangling earrings can be pulled through pierced ears.
- If glasses are worn plastic lenses will not shatter.
- A tight skirt is harder to run in than a more flowing one.
- Tuck scarfs into clothing, it may be less fashionable but it offers less to be clutched at.
- Tie back long hair to avoid it being grabbed.
- Carry a personal alarm which can be used to shock an assailant, so giving you time to run.

Record your movements

- Do not leave cryptic clues about your whereabouts. For example, 'Home visits – not returning', '10.00 am Mr Kipper', 'Clanhome estate and that area . . . not back', 'Visits . . . back at 2.00'.
- Do not just 'pop in' on a client on the way home, or because you are passing. Make sure someone knows where you are going, who you are going to see and when you will be back.

Exercise

1. In a small group identify the reasons why people in your team, group or workplace do not leave a record of their whereabouts. Discuss the legitimacy of the arguments given.

It is imperative that an adequate recording is kept of your whereabouts.
- Good practice dictates that people in the office have these details in order to pass on appropriate information to enquirers.
- You have an obligation to 'take reasonable care of your own safety' (Health and Safety at Work Act.)
- It could save your life.

Reporting back procedure

A reporting back procedure must be considered in conjunction with recording whereabouts, particularly where visits are protracted, or completed at the end of the day, in the evening or over the weekend. Knowing that you need to make a telephone call to a colleague following the visit will remove the fear that, should you be held against your will, or unable to leave because you have been harmed, no-one will know about your situation until the following day, or maybe even until after the weekend. Appropriate relatives of workers should be provided with a telephone contact to call if the worker fails to return home.

Client history

- Read the file if one exists.
- Make any appropriate telephone calls to gain information (hospital, GP, other agency, etc.).
- Has there been any previous contact with a colleague? If so talk to that colleague.

Time of visit

- Try to make all visits to potentially aggressive people during daylight hours. Daylight often gives a feeling of greater security to both worker and client.
- Where possible, complete such visits during working hours when it is easier to obtain assistance (e.g. being accompanied by another member of staff, reporting back etc.).
- Do not arrange a late afternoon visit if you have an early evening appointment, or want to get home early. Your mind may be on that and not on the situation in front of you.
- Identify when you are at your best and if you have the opportunity arrange the visit for then, you may be more alert in the morning or function better in the afternoon.
- If you know the client's situation you may be aware of something taking place in their lives which could affect the timing of this visit – a bereavement for example.
- Have you allowed enough time for the visit or will you be anxious that you have other appointments?
- Have you left a return time and itinerary with your colleagues?

Joint visit

- If you think that violence is likely during the visit take a colleague or go with the police: **Do NOT go alone**.

- If you think that violence is a possible outcome take all necessary and sensible precautions to ensure your safety.
- If you are in any way concerned that violence may occur do not go alone.
- If you go with the police, the roles are clear, i.e. you are there to complete your task and the police are there to keep the peace. It is possible that you will have to consider the effects upon the client of arriving with a police officer. You can either work through this at the time or at some later date. Remember that if there is a high risk of violence and there is no alternative to a home visit then that risk is reduced if you involve the police.

If you go with a colleague you must work out your roles beforehand. What do you expect of the colleague? Is the colleague effectively your bodyguard? Are you going as co-workers? Who does what during the interview should aggression occur?; if you are assaulted?; if you are threatened?; if you are shouted at?; if you are sworn at?; spat at?

Exercise

1. Do you think there is anything wrong with requesting a colleague to accompany you on a visit to a client with a known history of violence?

2. Is it viewed either by you, or by your peers, as a failure on the worker's part if such a request is made?

Environment

Consider the environment you will be visiting at two levels:

External

- State of repair, neatness, cleanliness of surrounding area and building being visited, a poor environment can affect self-esteem.
- Are there any deserted areas to walk through or avoid?
- Where will you park to ensure your safety? Too far away and you may not be able to reach the security of your vehicle.
- Do not worry about your vehicle – cars are replaceable, you are not.
- Look out for any local shops which, if open, may offer a place to run to if required.
- Look for any windows protected by grilles, bars or other forms. If so, does this suggest violence is more common in this area?
- Are there any public telephones? Vandalized? Phonecard?

Internal

- Are there steps to the door? Step down after knocking, at least one or two steps – moving away increases the distance between you and the person who opens the door as well as reducing the risk of being pushed.
- Will the door open inwards or outwards?
- If inwards, stand to one side so that you can clearly be seen as the door is opened.
- If outwards, step back.
- If the house is dark inside, ask for the light to be put on before entering.
- Be aware of the exits.
- Worn, holed carpets can trip you up, so too can loose wiring, obstacles etc., watch out for them on the way in.
- Try not to conduct your interview in a kitchen – or any place which offers easy access to knives, heavy implements and other weapons.
- Be aware of easily grabbed, heavy objects in the room, glass ashtrays can be used as weapons.
- Is there a dog in the house? Ask if it can be put into another room if you feel intimidated, or if it will impede the interview.
- Ask if the television can be turned off/down. Do not touch it yourself.
- If money is left close to you think about making a comment about it. Do not touch it.

Case study 4

It is 4.30 pm on a wintry evening. You have parked your car on the edge of the estate some 200–300 metres behind you. You are now walking between two high rise blocks of flats when you see a group of six youths clustered together by one block. You are close enough to recognize one of the youths as David Porter, a young lad who lives on the estate. His family are well known in the area with a reputation for being 'an aggressive lot' – most of the people on the estate are afraid of them. You do not recognize the others and think they must be lads from other estates.

The youths have obviously been drinking or sniffing glue (common to the estate). They are loud and boisterous and have overturned dustbins and sprayed cars and walls with paint. One of them, helped by a mate and encouraged by the others, is trying to break into the ground floor flat window of the elderly, anxious man you are to visit. You know the old man lives in fear on the estate – he has told you that his life is worthless, that he is afraid to go out – and you are immediately concerned that this act of hostility and aggression will seriously affect him.

Suddenly one of the group see you. *'There's that bastard from the council.'* You hear someone say. Three of the youths turn and start to walk towards you while the others remain still attempting to jemmy the window open. You hear the wooden frame snap.

1. What would be your immediate reaction?

2. What would you want to achieve and how could you achieve it?

3. What would be the possible consequences of your actions?

4. Role play the case study with your own responses.

11

Signalling Non-Aggression

When you are faced with an aggressor who may be shouting, threatening or jabbing a finger at you, or if you are being intimidated by someone who may be staring silently and threateningly at you, or facing any violent or aggressive situation, a number of physiological changes may take place within your body.

- Increased heart beat.
- Increased blood pressure.
- Raised blood glucose level.
- Breathing becomes more shallow.
- Increased rate of breathing.
- Increased flow of acids and digestive juices while digestive movements cease.
- Increased amounts of adrenalin, noradrenalin, cortisone and other hormones produced.
- Muscles contract as a preliminary to your next action.

It is these changes which cause the instinctive 'fight or flight' reaction. However, it is important to be aware that before 'fight or flight' can take place another stronger instinctive reaction can occur. Increasingly, evidence suggests that the most common reaction to threats of violence and/or aggression is that YOU FREEZE.

This freezing process may only be momentary, however, it is always significant. When this freezing is combined with the changes taking place in the non-verbal indications you give to the aggressor, which may be perceived as aggressive themselves, it becomes imperative that you signal non-aggression at an early stage in the interaction. The following is a list, by no means comprehensive, of ways of signalling non-aggression. These elements should be considered when facing an aggressive, abusive or angry person. They are *not* to be considered when faced with a situation of imminent physical violence, for example when someone is coming at you with an iron bar. There is another technique for dealing with this type of situation (*see* page 95).

How to signal non-aggression

1. **Control your breathing rate.** Inhale deeply and exhale slowly. This helps to increase a feeling of inner calmness and reduces panic and fear signals.
2. **Reduce the tension in your muscles**. As you breathe out slowly it becomes easier to relax the muscles around the neck. Concentrate on reducing the tension in your shoulders, which may have become hunched and threatening.
3. **Adopt a relaxed posture**. If standing, stand with your legs slightly apart, one foot slightly behind the other, turn to a slight angle to help reduce the element of face-to-face confrontation and place your weight on your back foot. This helps increase the distance from the aggressor and gives you the opportunity to move away rather than towards him/her.

4. **Use open hand language**. Hold your hands down, either at your sides or gently clasped in front of you. Occasionally, stress what you say with a slow, open hand gesture.

5. **Remain calm and aware of your communication skills**. Fear can be disabling but controlling the rate of your breathing helps to overcome this fear and increases personal security.

6. **Listen actively**. Reinforce your listening with occasional verbal affirmation *'hmmm/yes/ah, ha'* and head nods.

7. **Sit down**. This is not always easy to do, particularly if the aggressor is looming over you. However, by sitting down in a controlled manner you are indicating a willingness to stay and therefore stressing the importance of what the aggressor has to say. Furthermore, you are actively demonstrating a process of decreasing the aggressive atmosphere.

8. **Keep your voice low and steady**. This is not always easy, particularly when your vocal cords are tight and your throat dry. Once again slowing your rate of breathing helps to loosen the muscles around your neck and vocal cords, as well as giving you time to compose your reply rather than blurting out the first thing that comes to mind.

9. **Show you are interested and concerned**. This is the time to ask the 'How?' questions not the 'Why?' ones. *'How can I help you'* not *'Why are you like this?'*

10. **Empathize with the aggressor**. *'That sounds bad'* or *'I'd be angry too if it happened to me'*. Do this *only* if you are being sincere. Insincerity will be picked up and will escalate the situation.

11. **Ask for permission to make a note of what the aggressor is saying**. This helps to slow the aggressor down and stresses the importance of the information the aggressor has. This is a defusion technique as it moves from the act of aggression being expressed to what the aggressor has to say. (*see* also page 85.)

12. **Use eye movement**. Occasionally meeting the aggressor's eyes to stress or acknowledge a point will help, but always avert your eyes before a staring match develops.

Case study 5

You are driving home in your car. The car in front of you stops suddenly and you shunt into the back of it damaging the boot. The driver in the other car turns to his passenger and begins to shout furiously. He jumps out of his car and cursing he storms over to you angrily shaking his fist.

1. What would you do to signal non-aggression and to stop the situation from escalating?

2. Discuss your answers within a small group to identify the most appropriate method of dealing with the situation.

Possible solutions to case study 5

John had just shunted into the back of another car. The other driver was livid. Cursing, he slammed his door and strode purposefully towards John pointing his finger angrily, first at John and then at his car.

What was John to do? Drive off? The man would probably give chase. Get out of the car and face up to him, which could be interpreted as an aggressive act? Do nothing and allow the man to take it out on John's car? Literally, John's next move could be the difference between the situation escalating into violence or it cooling off into an expression of acceptable upsetness by the other, very irate driver.

Breathing in deeply John stayed seated in his car but wound the window down enough to speak through. Remaining seated he knew would signal non-aggression but it needed the additional act of winding the window down otherwise his inaction could have been viewed as a hostile act. He wound the window down as he hoped to signal to the other driver his willingness to talk about the accident. However, if he wound the window down too far John knew that a fist could be easily accessible.

He remained seated and as the other driver appeared at his window he leaned back a little, so increasing the distance between them. The other driver, still fuming, was now bent over John's car, his face inches away from the partly open window. *'Look what you've done you stupid bastard!'* he shouted. John was quaking inside and as a way of steadying his voice he took another deep breath before speaking. Then, in a sincere voice, keeping his tone serious and level he said, *'Yes, I'm sorry. Are you all right?'*

Apologizing is not the same as admitting liability (which can influence the insurance situation), but it is sometimes a powerful device to use; and by adding to this a show of concern for the other person, the aggression can be contained. *'Yeah. Yes. I'm all right,'* the man replied. *'It's . . . it's just my car . . . .'* His hunched shoulders relaxed as the aggression abated. Still keeping his voice at a low level John then said, *'I'll get out now so that we can check the damage,'* before he opened the door.

12

Defusion Techniques

There are a number of tried and tested methods of defusing an aggressive situation. Not all of these will work for everyone, nor will they all be appropriate to use in every aggressive situation. They are strategies to consider and to add to your range of skills. All of these defusion techniques may have the counter effect of escalating a situation. They require practice and use to ensure and maintain their value.

The techniques listed are in no particular order. Make use of the ones which you feel will work for you but practise them all with a friend or colleague to increase your range of techniques for dealing with dangerous situations.

- Divert.
- Distract.
- Request that the behaviour stops.
- Acknowledge that you have received the message.
- Consider humour.
- Sit down.
- Signal non-aggression.
- Express concern about the aggressor or his/her situation.
- Refer to past strengths.
- Remind the aggressor of what they have to lose.
- Maintain control of self.
- Leave.

Divert

This is a process of referring to, bringing in another subject, or refocusing attention.

Case study 6

An elderly man, confused after being recently admitted to an Elderly Persons' Home, became suddenly and unexpectedly agitated and disturbed. He stood upright, with his walking stick raised at the worker to whom he had been talking. Calmly and slowly the worker moved to the fireplace, keeping out of range of the stick.

'*Is this a picture of your cat?*' the worker asked motioning towards a framed picture standing there. The elderly man relaxed his stance as his mind was taken back to the fond memories he held about his pet. He smiled and lowered his stick.

Another method of diverting aggression is to offer to take notes of what is being said, with the intention of focusing the aggression on the content of the notes, and not the individual taking them. Then gradually slow down the rate at which the aggressor is giving the information. Try to include the aggressor in the process of forming the notes: *'OK now, how can I say/write that down'*, or *'Right, now what should I put down here?'*

Within child care a technique is used whereby a disturbed child is encouraged to hit a chair or cushion with a rolled up newspaper as a way of both identifying the depth of anger and diverting that anger on to an object. Maybe you can teach your aggressive clients a similar technique to divert anger from an individual?

Exercise

1. Identify any methods of diversion which you have used successfully.

Distract

This technique is similar to diversion, although perhaps a little more immediate. A simple example might be to look startled and ask *'What was that noise?'* or look around and firmly declare *'That's the police'*. Although this sounds simple, it is not, and requires practice to ensure that the conviction behind the expression is there. Without this conviction distraction will not work and the situation will escalate.

Alternatively, ask a colleague to listen for signs of escalation, and at that point knock on the interview room door, or call across the room saying *'There's a 'phone call for you!'*

A loud and unexpected noise (*see* 2-Stage Plan page 97) shouted into the face of an aggressor will also distract momentarily, thereby giving you the opportunity to run.

Request the behaviour stops

At an early stage ask the aggressor to stop the behaviour, *'Stop shouting and I'll see what I can do'*. By putting the behaviour into words it often helps the aggressor to gain a perception of what they are doing and the reply may be, *'I didn't realize I was shouting'*. If you do not request that the behaviour stop it may go on to a higher level until you do give some guidance as to what is, and what is not, acceptable behaviour.

Many people have been brought up to be polite with a desire to be liked and you may fear that it is impolite to be direct, or that you will be disliked if you make direct statements and demands about another person's behaviour. This can often lead you into the belief that you *did* request the behaviour to stop when in fact you said something like:

- *'That sort of behaviour isn't going to get you anywhere'*
- *'You won't be liked if you carry on like that'*
- *'Carrying on like that never helped anyone'*
- *'We can all stomp and shout, you know'*.

Be clear and direct in requesting the behaviour to stop. Make your request early on in the exhibition of behaviour. Use short sentences. Be positive in your offer to help once the behaviour has ceased. Give sanctions if necessary.

Exercise

1. Identify any indirect statements about behaviour that you make when you want aggressive behaviour to stop.

2. Practise making direct statements about aggressive behaviour.

Acknowledge you have received the message

By making a statement about the aggressive behaviour, you are telling the aggressor that you have received the message they are sending to you. You are also informing them that they do not need to escalate the situation in order to ensure a response from you.

If you ignore an expression of anger it will generally increase in intensity until you do address it. *'I can see you are angry by the way you're shouting'*, or *'You don't have to shout'*, followed up with a positive statement can often help – *'You don't have to shout for me to help you.'* Occasionally the perceived aggression may be no more than a misinterpretation on your part – *'I wasn't shouting, I talk like this because I'm deaf.'*

Humour

A cajoling form of humour may be useful, particularly if you know the aggressor. However do not attempt humour at the expense of the aggressor. A light hearted, *'Come on Dave, this isn't like you'*, making use of warmth in your voice and a gentle, warm smile may help.

Other forms of humour have been known to work, in particular making a joke about the method chosen by the aggressor, *'he looked and sounded just like a monkey so I started making noises like one and jumping around and very soon we were both in absolute fits of laughter'*, or *'I couldn't help it. I didn't think about doing it. I just raised my eyebrows and made a funny face and we both curled up laughing'*. The use of such humour when faced with an aggressive person is always dangerous and should only be tried if you normally feel comfortable with its use.

Sit down

Sitting down is a good way of defusing a situation, and of actually taking the situation down a level. It is also perhaps the hardest thing to do in a situation where the natural tendency is to want to 'stand up to it' or to 'face it head on'. *Do not* sit down if you feel insecure in doing so or if physical violence is imminent.

The manner in which you sit down is important. You do not want to signal 'victim' to the aggressor, and you want to signal that you are in control. It is important to sit down yourself before requesting the aggressor to sit. When you do move remember to keep your movements as fluid and purposeful as possible – do not move suddenly to sit down. Explain to the aggressor what you are doing, perhaps saying *'Let's sit down to talk about this'*, using open hand language to offer the aggressor an available chair.

Exercise

1. List the violent incidents that you have some knowledge of and identify those that took place when: both parties were standing and when one or both parties were seated.

Signal non-aggression

Make use of the techniques already outlined.

Express concern about the aggressor or his/her situation

Expressing empathy, acknowledging the awfulness or the powerlessness of the aggressor's situation or plight often proves to be an important element in defusing situations, *'If I was in your place I'd be angry too'*.

Refer to past strengths

By referring to previous situations (if known), where the aggressor succeeded you can drawn on, and reawaken, the aggressor's positive self-image. *'When you came in last week we were able to do x and x. You didn't have to shout then to get things done and you don't have to today'*.

Remind aggressor of what they have to lose

This technique may reintroduce reality and gives the aggressor the opportunity to weigh up the possible outcomes. Try *'I can't help you if you continue to . . .'*, or *'If you continue to shout I'll leave'*, or *'I can see you're angry but if you don't stop now, I will telephone the police'*, or *'If you hit me you will end up in court'*, or *'Stop (the behaviour) or you will have to leave'*.

However, do not use threats of sanctions which you cannot, or which you do not intend to carry through. If you do propose a sanction, as a way of reminding the aggressor of what they have to lose, and the aggression is still maintained *you must then carry out the threatened sanction*.

Maintain control of self

If you can contain your own anxieties and fears, and retain some control over your non-verbal messages, then you can play a constructive part in helping the aggressor to contain their fear and anxiety.

- Regulate breathing.
- Use slower body movements.
- Keep your voice at a low level.
- Use open hand language.
- Retain a relaxed posture.

Give the aggressor a positive message and a positive role model. This can help the aggressor to reintroduce the lost boundaries and stop the process of feeding into and increasing the level of anxiety.

Leave

This should be the first consideration for anyone who is faced with an aggressor. Furniture and fittings are replaceable – *you are not*. There are a number ways of leaving:

- arrange to see the person again after a breathing space, thus allowing the aggression to dissipate
- let the person know why you are leaving
- offer to make some tea/to get something from the car
- arrange for the person to see someone else
- arrange for a colleague to interrupt with a message such as an 'urgent telephone call'
- back out slowly
- walk away, shepherding any people for whom you are responsible
- run.

Remember, you are not being paid to be a hero. There is nothing wrong with leaving a situation in order to plan and re-think a strategy. A strategic withdrawal is the military definition. Think about it. Do it.

Do not hold on to the belief that you are responsible for the office furniture if someone is wrecking it.

Do not believe that you are responsible for ensuring that the items in your possession must be protected at the cost of your life.

You are responsible for yourself and, in many instances, for people in your care. By leaving, you ensure your own safety and maintain your responsibility towards others by remaining alive and uninjured. In this state you are able to make use of alternative strategies, such as seeking assistance from others, calling the police, removing others from the area etc. If you are damaged you fail those around you, leaving them vulnerable.

Remember all of these defusion techniques are possible escalation points; their appropriate usage needs practise. Make use of those techniques which you feel comfortable with and practise their use with a friend or colleague.

Exercise

To be done in groups of three. Each participant to consider an act of aggression which concerned them. Hand out cards A, B and C which identify the parts to be played.

A = the aggressor

B = the subject of the aggression

C = the observer.

- Each participant in turn to take each of the above parts.
- Participant 'A' gives an account of the incident in which they were concerned and then assumes the role of the aggressor.
- Participant 'B' assumes the part of the subject and either attempts to escalate or defuse the aggression.
- Participant 'C' observes the interaction. Notes down and watches for pointers which escalate and elements which defuse the aggression.

Each playlet takes approximately five minutes and is followed by feedback from the observer plus a discussion of the feelings involved by both participants.

- The process continues until all three participants have taken all parts.

This exercise allows all participants the freedom of trying out defusion techniques in a controlled situation. It often leads to a greater understanding of the elements which gave rise to aggressive behaviour, as it asks for each participant to consider the behaviour involved by both the aggressor and the 'victim'. The exercise should be followed by a group discussion to allow for learning points to be discussed within the group and for further debriefing.

13

Handling Acts of Violent and Aggressive Behaviour

Within your work you will deal with the most complicated and complex of creatures – human beings. Each one is different and each one is likely to react differently if placed in a similar situation. Therefore it is not possible to offer a magical solution on how to handle a violent and/ or aggressive person which will work in every case. Be prepared to discover that what may work within one situation or with one client may not work as well, or indeed, at all, with another.

This chapter concentrates upon methods of surprise, defusing and calming acts of violence and aggression. There are a number of other methods available for handling violent and aggressive acts, however, the methods used in this chapter are known for their simplicity and commonsense value. Like any technique they will require practise, and in practising them you may discover that these techniques are not appropriate for you to make use of for some reason. Try to find out now before you are faced with the real situation. The techniques proposed are:

- a 2-stage plan for dealing with acts of imminent physical violence
- a 6-stage plan for handling aggression
- an assertive strategy.

Remember that no matter how skilled you are or how many techniques you may have available for dealing with the behaviour, sometimes nothing will work. The aggressor may be so determined to damage something or someone that your skills will be of no use. Fortunately, although these situations do occur they are infrequent and the techniques outlined are ones which do work.

Before considering these methods however, it is important to take account of some of the other components which have an influence upon the handling of the situation.

Are you having a good or bad day?

The type of day you are having has an affect upon the way you handle a situation. On a good day everything may be going your way, on a bad one you cannot do anything right and may therefore be less receptive to escalating signs, or your judgement of a situation may not be as accurate.

If you are having a 'bad' day try to stay away from aggressive situations. If you cannot, try taking some time out to rest, reflect and compose yourself before the interaction.

Are you tired, overloaded, burntout, stressed?

These factors can alter your perception, slow your reactions and reduce your capacity to deal effectively with situations of conflict. Slow down, reduce your workload, take a break from work.

Lack of support

If there is no-one to discuss the potential risks with you may go into situations unprepared. If you cannot discuss the emotions generated before and after the event your opportunities for learning from it are reduced. Seek out supervision, use the 'buddy' system or bring like-minded colleagues together to form support groups. Organize a system of support now before an incident, do not wait until an incident occurs.

Chance

Always remember that chance plays its part and sometimes it is just bad luck, or good fortune, that the situation did or did not become violent, or that you were called or not called upon to intervene.

Consider methods of increasing the odds in your favour.

- Carry a personal alarm in an accessible place.
- Walk in well-lit areas.
- Try not to be in a building on your own.
- Do not deal with potentially violent people by yourself.
- Get some training in what to do in violent situations.

Carry-over of emotions

Anger, annoyance and frustration are all emotions which you can carry from one person or situation and dump on to another. Your clients may do the same. Think about it. Who are you angry with? Take time to let the feeling go away – have a breath of fresh air. If you find yourself expressing anger inappropriately, apologize.

Remember that your clients can also carry-over emotions and may 'dump' them on you. Do not over-react. Do not react to verbal abuse as a personal attack. Do not ignore it but do not escalate a situation by rowing.

Attitude

Although there is no excuse for violence, the attitude of the worker can be a contributory factor to the escalation of a situation from an expression of anger into one of violence. Consider the following and draw your own conclusions:

- *'he was so patronizing, it really wound me up'*
- *'it was the offhand way he had'*
- *'it was really so thoughtless what was said'*
- *'it was obvious that he didn't care about me. He had his job to do and he was going to do it regardless of my feelings'*
- *'look, I know they were busy. I just wanted someone, anyone to stop and listen, to talk to me for a minute. That was all'*
- *'I suppose I thought I'd better get down there and sort it out, after all he was my client'*

- *'he was in the kitchen rattling knives and things and I knew I couldn't let him get away with that'*
- *'these people, they're all the same. Try to show them a little bit of respect and they laugh in your face'*
- *'I've dealt with this type all my life'*
- *'nothing that I'm going to do will have any effect whatsoever'*
- *'I can handle it'.*

It is necessary to consider your attitude towards the client both before and during the contact, remembering that non-verbal information is being received during every interaction.

Workplace culture

If the culture within your workplace is based on criticism, or simply one where feelings are not discussed, it becomes difficult to express fears or anxieties about handling a situation. You are led to believe that an expression of feeling, often so necessary to reduce anxiety, is viewed by management and colleagues as a weakness.

Unexpressed anxiety can become a disabling force

Exercise

1. Consider the culture which exists within your workplace. Is it supportive? If not what can you do to make it more so?

Winding-up your clients

At some time everyone winds someone up, either purposefully or inadvertently. Become aware of the way *you* do it. Think about the things you do which wind-up your clients and make a list. Your list might look something like this:

- ignore them altogether
- talk across them to another person
- shout out their personal details in a crowded room

- dismiss what they are saying
- lie to them
- keep them waiting
- fail to apologize
- deny their importance
- make them look or feel small
- humiliate them
- give them indifferent attention
- wear a smirk
- wag a finger.

This, and your list (which may contain elements more appropriate to your setting), *must* be regarded as a list of do not's when dealing with an aggressive person.

These then are some of the factors which have an influence on your ability to deal effectively with violent and aggressive clients. The following techniques may help as basic guidelines for handling the behaviour which you may face.

A 2-stage plan for dealing with violence

It is important to remember that a common reaction to violent and aggressive behaviour is freezing. This replaces the commonly held theory of the instant reaction being either flight or fight.

Freezing occurs for a number of reasons:
- disbelief.
- shock.
- surprise.
- questions running through your mind.
- fear.

The list is almost endless. However, it is the non-action – the freezing – which must be countered.

To actively counter freezing, you must actually do something to snap yourself into action, to give the fight-or-flight reaction the opportunity to take place, immediately following a breakthrough in the freezing barrier. The 2-stage plan is simple and consists of:
- stage 1: break the freezing process
- stage 2: action.

However, it does require practise.

Exercise

Close your eyes and imagine you are alone on a deserted train station platform one Sunday afternoon. You have just been visiting a friend and have thoughts of the morning in your mind. Out of the corner of your eye you see some movement. You turn and are confronted by a potential mugger no more than 15 metres away,

striding towards you carrying an iron bar raised above his head.
   Individually or with a partner decide:

1: How would you respond?

2. What would you do next?

3. What would be the possible outcomes of your next move?

As the mugger approaches to within about two metres you shout at the top of your voice '*Dee Dah! Dee Dah! Dee Dah!*' Individually or with a partner:

1. What do you think the effect on the mugger will be?

2. What do you think the effect on yourself will be?

This two tone shout is a surprise technique which is increasingly being used in North America. There they now consider that the two tone shout has more effect than a scream would because it is unusual and unexpected. Two factors should be remembered before suggesting this shout.
1. Many people find it difficult to scream in public. There are a number of restrictions – many related to upbringing.
2. In North America particularly a scream is so commonplace that its shock value has been eroded.
Shouting this two tone noise will have two effects:
1. The attacker will be stunned, confused or surprised and this momentary shock will be enough to stop him/her in his/her tracks.
2. This overt act will break the freezing process giving you the opportunity to act; and because your body has experienced physiological changes (increased adrenalin etc) you will be able to make use of this by running, or taking some other action.
   Running is advocated because any form of physical action against the attacker on your part could end up in either harming him/her or you being harmed. You could even find yourself the subject of a criminal assault charge.
   Using the voice to break the freezing process may not be something that everyone can do. Like any other strategic approach, it requires practise. Try out the noise for yourself. Hear what it sounds like, become accustomed to it. Do not rely upon being able to do it should you be attacked. Remember a common reaction to violence is freezing.

Exercise

1. With a partner think up a number of case studies and practise making the two tone noise, or some other noise, as a method of shocking your would be attacker. Discuss the impact on the 'assailant' of the different noises you make up.

If you ever have to distract an aggressor who may, for example, be attacking a colleague, try shouting that the police are coming, dousing him/her in cold water (a fire extinguisher for example can be used) or making some other loud noise (e.g. slamming a door). However, the shock effect will be short-lived and may attract the aggressor's attention to yourself. Be prepared to run.

If you are grabbed by the aggressor, using physical force may be your only recourse. In these circumstances whatever you choose to do, do it quickly. If you do it quickly you will do it with strength and it is feasible that with a sudden swift movement you will break the aggressor's hold long enough for you to run.

You can attend a course on self-defence in order to learn some techniques for breaking holds. Remember, however, that any training must be repeated regularly so that you do not forget the techniques.

Personal alarms

If you feel that you are unable to use the two tone shout, consider carrying a personal alarm which, if used appropriately, can have a similar shock effect.

Personal alarms are usually small enough to fit into a pocket – some are flat, some cylindrical. They emit a high-pitched screech to distract the attacker and attract other people to your situation. Although they may not bring people to your assistance personal alarms can distract the aggressor long enough for you to make your escape.

A personal alarm is only effective if it is readily accessible. They are valueless if tucked away (e.g. in a handbag or briefcase) and take a few seconds of fumbling around to find. They are also dangerous if worn on a cord around your neck as this provides the attacker with something to hold. Try attaching one to a belt around your waist; sticking a piece of velcro to one with another piece on the inside of a coat or jacket; carrying one in an inside coat pocket, or even in your hand ready to use if necessary. Some alarms can be connected to a wrist strap and automatically activated should the alarm be snatched.

If you do purchase a personal alarm, test it regularly, (at least once every two to three months) to make sure it still works. Gas ones may leak or be subject to evaporation; in battery operated ones the battery may fail. To test the alarm, it is advisable to choose an open space – testing indoors (particularly in a closed room) may damage hearing. To test gas filled alarms hold the alarm at arms length with the nozzle pointing away from the body and gently press the top, release after a second. Battery operated alarms have a switch which needs to be pressed.

Caution: Do not place yourself at risk simply because you feel more secure carrying a personal alarm.

The following method is a strategic plan to handle verbal aggression, threats or abuse in a one-to-one situation. It can be used to calm down an aggressive person. It is not to be considered where physical assault is imminent. In such circumstances use the 2-Stage Plan previously outlined, one of the methods of removing yourself from the situation (*see* page 90), or summon help from colleagues, police etc.

A 6-stage plan for dealing with aggression

1. Stay calm and signal non-aggression.
2. Show concern.
3. Acknowledge the manner of expressed aggression.
4. Defuse the situation.
5. Identify the cause(s) and seek solution(s).
6. Renegotiate the relationship.
Stages can be interchanged and you do not have to use all the stages to calm the aggressor.

Stage 1: Stay calm and signal non-aggression

This is not an easy thing to do particularly when physiological changes in your body such as a pounding heart, increased and more shallow breathing rate, quivering speech, dry throat, muscle tenseness of the trunk and limbs etc, occur and may be seen as fear or aggression. At the same time psychological changes in your perceptions may be creating the freezing process.
   To enable a feeling of calmness and to signal non-aggression:
- take a deep breath and exhale slowly before speaking. This action will automatically allow the tension in the shoulders and neck to ease and free up the vocal cords. Secondly, it helps to instill a feeling of inner calm and control which is so necessary and finally, it allows time to think of your response
- keep movements slow and use open hand language
- sit down and invite the aggressor to sit also
- actively listen.

Stage 2: Show concern

Again this is not easy when, reactively, you may be thinking '*I want to give as good as I get*', or '*this is nothing to do with me*', or even, '*how dare you!*' Remove thoughts such as these from your mind. Your job is to deal with the aggressive behaviour irrespective of the circumstances.

1. Assume that there is a reason for the behaviour and that you want to find out the reason for it.
2. Ask 'How' and/or 'What' questions not 'Why' ones. For example, *'How can I help'*, *'What can I do?'*
3. Keep your tone of voice light and even.
4. Establish eye contact but *do not* stare.
5. Use occasional head nods to signify that you are listening.
6. Empathize. Try to see the world from the aggressor's viewpoint. How would you feel if you were facing his/her problems/dilemmas?
7. Express this empathy.

Stage 3: *Acknowledge the manner of expressed aggression*

By putting the actions of the aggressor into words you enable those actions to be reconsidered by the aggressor who may not be aware of the way s/he is being perceived. Also, by stating your perception you are able to clarify any false assumptions or misconceptions.

If you fail to acknowledge a message being given to you then that message will continue to be given, probably increasing in intensity until acknowledgement is given.

There are a number of ways of acknowledging the expressed aggression. For example: *'I can see you're angry'*, *'stop shouting'*, *'please don't swear'*, *'I don't know what you want me to do when you get so threatening/intimidating'*. Do *not* say *'I can understand how you feel'*.

Stage 4: *Defuse the situation*

You may have chosen to use this method earlier. Use one or more of the defusion techniques already outlined (*see* page 85).

Stage 5: *Identify the cause(s) and seek solution(s)*

Once the aggressor has calmed down you can ask the 'Why' questions. Now is the time to consider the reasons which led to the expression of aggression. It may be that the reason(s) are intangible and difficult to identify or they may be easily identified but difficult to change.

If the problem is clearly identified it becomes necessary to move into resolution strategies with the client. If not, more time needs to be spent to allow for problem exploration. Remember, that some problems may not be identified and others may not have a solution. At this stage it is important to be seen in a supportive role and not an accusatory one.

Seek solutions with the person concerned but if none are to be found it is important that (if possible) this is jointly identified, or that this information is shared with the now calmed aggressor. This stage may be achievable within the initial interaction. However, it may also take considerable time to accomplish.

Stage 6: *Renegotiate the relationship*

Once the aggression has eased and the situation is calm, it becomes necessary to re-examine the relationship which now exists between you and the aggressor. It is no good assuming that everything will be as it was before the aggressive incident. If, for example, the aggressor threatened to kill you, you need to be aware of where you now stand before any further work or isolated contact with the aggressor takes place.

This renegotiation can take place immediately following the calming down of the aggressor, or a later date. If you choose the later date, choose a safe place to do the renegotiation, or take someone with you if you need to see the person in their own home or in a place not considered safe.

The renegotiation may be as simple as: *'Last week when you were so angry you said you were going to get me. How do you feel about that now?'* Although it may not provide a concrete answer as to whether the aggression will take place again or not; it does allow you to consider fresh information concerning further interactions between yourself and the person concerned.

No doubt you will recognize elements within this 6-stage plan that you already make use of. It is a commonsense approach which will help handle aggressive situations.

Exercise

1. With a partner consider an aggressive situation in which you were involved. Identify any of the above six stages which you made use of in order to calm the aggressor down.

2. Discuss with a partner what could have been the outcome had you applied the 6-stage plan to your situation.

Assertive responses

To be assertive is to practise a form of communicating which is neither aggressive nor passive. Assertiveness is the middle road which leads to clear, honest and direct communication. It is not a form of communication which everyone makes use of, nor one which everyone will feel comfortable with. However, assertive communication can be used as a strategy for dealing with aggressive behaviour.

There are a number of pointers which everyone can make use of and which form the basis for assertive communication:

1. **Be clear**:
   - about what you want
   - about what you want to say
   - about your purpose, i.e. to stop the aggression from escalating
   - about what you are, and are not, prepared to accept.
2. **Be precise**:
   - use short sentences, repeating them if necessary. When the aggressor is in a highly charged, emotional state clear, short messages will be heard better than long, involved ones.
3. **Be specific**:
   - address the issue of aggression before you. Other issues will wait, this one will not. Do not assume the aggressor will know they are being aggressive – make a clear statement about the expression of aggression, '*Stop shouting and I will try to help*'.
4. **Be direct**:
   - often you assume it is impolite to be direct. If you want the behaviour to stop it is no good casting your eyes to the ceiling and sighing heavily, hoping the aggressor will understand you. Request the behaviour stops.
5. **Be positive**:
   - in both what you say and what you do. If you do not know the answer do not feel that you have to make something up. Say you do not know, but that you can find out or can direct the person to someone who does know
   - give positive body messages – open hand gestures, no sudden movements, relaxed posture etc.
6. **Be confident**:
   - in your skills and abilities. Do not allow the disabling effects created when facing an act of aggression to deskill you. Remind yourself that you are an able communicator.

Always remember that facing aggression and violence can cause even the most experienced worker to freeze. A frightening situation is one which often disables the most competent worker. Remain aware that in your job you actively communicate with people who may be angry or express aggression. You will be dealing with such people on a day-to-day basis; do not allow the fear of aggressive behaviour rob you of the skills you already have for communicating with people.

Assertive strategy

1. Stay calm – take a deep breath, listen carefully to what is being said.
2. Request behaviour to stop and offer help '*Stop shouting. I'll try to help.*' If the aggression continues:

3. Respond empathetically and assertively *'I'd be angry too if this happened to me. Stop shouting. I want to help.'* If the aggression continues:

4. State difficulties and repeat offer to help *'I can't help if you continue to shout. Stop shouting. I want to help.'* If the aggression continues:

5. Express the effect of aggression upon your ability to resolve the situation *'Your shouting is making me feel anxious. I can't help you if I'm like this. Stop shouting and I will try to help.'* If the aggression continues:

6. Break off interaction. Arrange to meet or telephone at a later date. *'Let's both take a break. We're not getting anywhere.'*

Assertive people tend to have certain qualities which help in handling aggressive situations and which everyone can make use of. Assertive people:

- are not afraid to say they do not know
- are not drawn into inappropriate rows
- are able to control their immediate responses
- admit to being human
- apologize for making a mistake
- give more positive messages than negative ones
- communicate clearly and concisely
- do not make promises they cannot keep
- maintain high self-esteem
- do not seek conflict, nor maintain it
- are able to say how they feel
- criticize the behaviour not the individual
- recognize other people's needs
- recognize their own needs
- understand that there does not have to be a winner and a loser
- maintain a basic belief in the integrity of fellow humans.

Case study 7

You are working late, using a colleague's office, trying to get a report finished and are unaware of the time. You look at your watch and are surprised to find that it is 6.30 pm. The office is deserted by this time. You begin to pack up. Suddenly the door to the office opens and a man whom you do not know is standing in the doorway. He sways a little and it's obvious to you that he's been drinking. You can smell the alcohol on his breath from where you are behind the desk. *'You're all the same,'* he drawls sarcastically. *'You lot did it'*, his voice begins to rise. *'It's all your fault.'* He points a finger at you accusingly and starts to enter the office.

1. Decide what you would do next and why.

2. In a group, role play the scene and discuss the way the situation could have escalated and what technique the worker could have used to handle the aggression.

Summary

1. **Use short sentences**: if a person is in a highly charged emotional state short statements are more likely to be heard than long, rambling ones.
2. **Be specific**: refer to the behaviour. Do not assume that the aggressor will be aware of their actions. Request the behaviour to stop.
3. **Be clear**: do not become drawn into an argument at this point. Remember that it is the aggressive behaviour which you want to defuse, that is your focus, once the behaviour has been calmed you can then consider the information being given.
4. **Know what you want and say it**: do not assume that the aggressor will know that you want the behaviour to cease. Until you actually say 'stop' how will the aggressor know that their message has been received?
5. **Repeat your point if necessary**: when the aggressor is in a highly charged emotional state it becomes difficult to receive messages and the first, second or even third message will go unheeded.
6. **Demonstrate that you are actively listening**: nod occasionally, seek eye contact, repeat the important parts of what the aggressor is saying back to him/her.
7. **Say how you feel**: if you feel threatened, afraid, anxious, etc., your body language will probably demonstrate this to the aggressor. However, often stating the way you feel can give you an inner strength. Furthermore, the aggressor will see *and hear* the effect his or her actions are having and this gives the aggressor the opportunity to decide to either continue or amend their behaviour.
8. **Leave**: always remember *you* are the important thing to consider. You can always leave a situation and then determine a strategy to handle your return, or another strategy for dealing with it before you are damaged.

14

The Responsibilities of Line Managers

Every staff manager has a responsibility to enable their staff to perform their duties as comprehensively as possible. To, in effect, get the best out of their staff. This benefits both the organization and the individual.

Within this there are clearly identifiable areas of responsibility to consider regarding violence encountered by staff while in the performance of their duties:

- legislative responsibilities
- responsibility to support staff
- providing a safe working environment
- ensuring adequate recording
- attitudes
- reporting procedures
- policy statements.

Legislation

Employers have a responsibility, often vested within their managers, under the Health and Safety at Work Act 1974 to reduce the risk of violence to staff. *'It shall be the duty of every employer to ensure, so far as is reasonably practicable, the health, safety and welfare at work of all his employees.'* (Section 2).

Whilst it is the responsibility of the employee to *'take reasonable care for their own and others' safety'*, the employer has a legal duty to provide a safe working environment and to devise and maintain safe working practices. Employers may be liable to criminal proceedings if this duty is ignored or not considered. Appropriate safe working practices include the provision of safety equipment, training, adequate levels of supervision and disciplinary procedures.

The role of the manager is crucial in ensuring that the obligations of the employer to her/his employees are met and vice versa.

Employees must be allowed to identify when violent and aggressive situations are encountered, and managers must ensure that resistance to the reporting of incidents, unfortunately all too commonplace, is overcome. The manager becomes the focal point through which the needs, to ensure the safety of employees, are identified and provided.

'Where violent incidents are foreseeable employers have a duty under Section 2 of the Health and Safety at Work Act, to identify the nature and extent of the risk and to devise measures which provide a safe workplace and a safe system of work. . . All managers must take every threat of violence seriously. So must all staff and contractors. Employees should be encouraged (by managers) to report threats as well as physical abuse and become confident that action will be taken (by managers) on their behalf. No-one should stay silent out of fear of reprisal, misplaced sense of guilt or personal failure. Managers must ensure that their staff are aware of the support which will be made available and training has a particular importance in this context.' Report of the DHSS Advisory Committee on Violence to Staff. HMSO, 1988.

Exercise

In a small group or as an individual complete the following and present the findings to your management for discussion.
1. What levels of violence are tolerated, and therefore institutionalized, within your work environment?

	At your place of work	On home visits	Elsewhere
1.			
2.			
3.			
4.			
5.			
6.			

Staff support

Time and time again similar messages are repeated by various staff about their managers.
- *'You've forgotten what it feels like to be a worker'.*
- *'Your "macho/it's all part of the job" approach really doesn't help'.*
- *'You individualize and accuse when you investigate the circumstances of the assault'.*
- *'The job is harder than when you did it'.*
- *'You're never here'.*
- *'You're not supportive'.*
- *'Take a walk around the area, see it, feel it, remind yourself of what you're expecting me to do every day'.*
- *'We're different people and the level of behaviour you can, or did tolerate, is different to the level of behaviour which affects me'.*

- 'You expect a lot and criticize when I get it wrong. That's fine so long as you remember to praise when I get it right!'
- 'Just whose side are you on anyway?'

Case study 8

A member of your team/staff has been involved in a violent incident and upon returning to work (following annual leave) you receive the following information:

Susan Dalea, who has been employed for four months, and is therefore still in her probationary period, is at home following an incident which occurred 10 days ago, shortly after your leave began.

Susan had visited David McLocklan, the father of one of her cases, on three occasions (the file is not up to date and you are not aware of the reason for these visits). On Tuesday (10th) Mr McLocklan called into the workplace at 2.00 pm. He had been drinking and was annoyed at being kept waiting. Susan returned from lunch at 2.20 and immediately invited Mr McLocklan into the interview room. After a few minutes raised voices were heard coming from the interview room and almost immediately following this Susan came running from the room grasping the neck of her dress which had been torn. Mr McLocklan left the building and has not been seen since.

Susan had run into the kitchen and was comforted there by the receptionist. The managers, who were all involved in an urgent priority meeting at Head Office, had left a telephone number for emergencies and upon being contacted by the receptionist the Duty Manager suggested Susan be taken home. This the receptionist did.

The Duty Manager, upon returning to the office, left this message in your notebook '10th. Tuesday. 4.45 pm. Susan Dalea sent home after being assaulted by one of her clients (Mr McLocklan). She was distressed. Thought it for the best. She'll probably need to talk to you about it – tried to fill in the incident form for you but haven't got all the facts. Hope she's OK. Hope you had a nice holiday.'

The duty manager went off with 'flu on Wednesday 11th. You have two other pieces of information:

1. Susan was late returning from lunch following a visit to the 'local' where she was taken for a celebratory 'welcome to the area' drink. She had two drinks (two halves of cider). This 'welcome drink' is something that you have normally encouraged within the group.
2. Susan had been involved in a violent incident in her previous job. You understand from a friend that the findings of the internal inquiry which followed suggested that she may have 'dressed inappropriately' while interviewing certain clients.

There has been no contact with Susan since she was taken home 10 days ago.

1. As Susan's manager draw up a plan of action.

2. What needs to be done now and why?

Important considerations for staff support

- Violent incidents can rob the worker of esteem, security and a belief in self, allow for this and be prepared to discuss it openly.
- Allow time and space for the healing process.
- Make yourself aware of the effects of violence upon the victim.
- Refer to past strengths as a method of rebuilding confidence.
- Consider implementation of strategies to protect staff from repetition of incident.
- Consider a variety of strategies to reduce the potential for violence occurring.
- Encourage debriefing, a time to allow for the worker to describe in detail the events of the incident and their feelings etc. (*see* page 24 debriefing model).
- Schedule time to discuss any incident, ensuring that this arrangement is viewed as a part of the culture of the workplace.
- Visit the worker at home in order to discuss the effects upon him/her or simply to find out how s/he is.
- Telephone your worker to ask how s/he is.
- Be aware of practical issues such as insurance and compensation issues, sick leave, access to counselling, legal advice etc.
- Consider with the worker an appropriate return to work and plan it out.
- Be prepared to reallocate work duties on a temporary or permanent basis – ensure the worker is aware of this and of the reasons behind it.
- Make reallocation a part of the agency culture prior to an incident.
- Encourage and allow support from the team or working group.
- Where acceptable and appropriate consider approaching and involving the victim's family.
- Consider the other people involved in the incident and decide if they need any support/ information or practical assistance.
- Discourage staff from drinking alcohol during the lunch break.
- Ensure the incident is recorded as per your agency policy.
- Report incidents to the police and, if required, improve contacts with them.
- Monitor incidents to identify trends in location, types of violence, employee groups more likely to experience it, contributory factors etc., in order to improve and update procedures and policies.
- Periodically reassess the policies and practice which exist for reducing the potential for violence and for protecting staff and improve as required.
- Remind yourself you are not expected to get everything right, and on occasion, no matter how much you try it will not be enough. You are not a magician. The important thing is that you try.

Safe working environment?

- *'There are some estates I'm expected to work on where the police have refused to go'.*
- *'They do provide parking. It's a multi-storey. We've got the basement. It's dark and quite frankly at night sometimes I'm terrified, particularly when I've just been threatened by a client'.*
- *'There are no lights outside. I lock up. I'm alone. The place is deserted. Sometimes one or two people are hanging about near the door. Last week we had to send someone home because he was acting strangely.*

He was there outside, waiting when I left. He didn't do anything. He was just angry but it worries me sometimes, after all these people are here because there's something wrong with them'.

- 'We've got no panic buttons. Anyway I don't think they'd be used even if we did have them.'
- 'The last time I pressed the panic alarm they thought it was the fire bell. By the time someone realized it wasn't, he'd gone. But anything could have happened.'
- 'You know what really frightened me, the fact that I made use of the panic alarm and it made no difference. No-one came, well not immediately. I've stopped feeling safe.'
- 'I'm supposed to take this kid in my car by myself. Everyone knows he's been violent in the past but they say we've got to show we trust him. That's all well and good but what about me? What if something happens?'
- 'During the day there's four or five staff around, but at night it's just me. Yes, OK, so they are asleep, but there's 14 of them and just one night staff. Anything could happen. When I said this to my supervisor she gave me a list of telephone numbers and said to 'phone if I needed help.'
- 'There's just not enough staff to always do joint visits even when you know it's a risky one. People don't like always being asked. And it's always the same ones who get asked.'
- 'I just popped in on my way home. Thought I'd do it so it wouldn't nag at me over the weekend. I was really scared. No-one knew I was there. She kept the scissors at my neck for a good hour. It was only when her son came back from the disco that I was able to get away. I didn't tell anyone. I left soon after that.'
- 'It's because I'm so big. Whenever there's any aggro, they call on me. I suppose it's because everyone thinks I can handle myself. I don't really mind but I wish they'd understand that it affects me too.'

Exercise

1. As a group of managers, identify in a brainstorm the different tasks/parts of the job which you expect your staff to perform.

2. Break down these job tasks into their different constituent parts. For example, home visits can be broken down into the more precise categories of:
   - to people with a known history of unpredictable behaviour
   - to people with a known history of violence
   - to remove a child into care
   - to provide emotional support in bereavement
   - to a particular area, block of flats or estate
   - completed on the way home, in the dark and so forth.

3. Now place each of these constituent parts under one of the following headings:

Little or no risk identified	Possibility of some violence		Probability of violence	
	LOW	HIGH	LOW	HIGH

Complete this process for each employee type/group for whom you are responsible. Once completed you will have a comprehensive picture which will indicate the areas where immediate action should be taken to reduce the possibility of violence to your staff. In particular all those areas identified under the high probability heading will require some attention. Similarly, although with less priority, those which appear under the high possibility heading will also require attention.

You may like to ask your staff to consider a similar exercise on each of the cases which they consider pose some risk. By breaking down the tasks involved you enable workers to identify safer working practices with 'higher risk' clients.

4. Individually, walk around the environment in which your staff work. Identify all those elements which may increase the possibility of violence occurring and those which decrease the possibility. Now join together with your peer group to share those elements which you have identified as possibly reducing violence and identify possible solutions for the rest. Refer your findings to senior management.

Recording

Most agencies have a procedure for recording violent incidents and/or aggressive behaviour. Part of the manager's task is to ensure that these procedures are followed and that any recordings made are of an adequate standard to allow the information to be acted upon.

None of the following statements contain enough information to allow for appropriate action to deal with or reduce the possibility of violence. This is to the detriment of both the client concerned and any future worker relying upon the case recording. Yet these statements, and many similar ones, have stood alone on the files of the people concerned for a number of years. *'David has a history of violent and aggressive behaviour. This behaviour can be traced back to his early childhood when he was assessed as being "an aggressive, truculent and moody child"'*, *'she has a history of violent behaviour'*, *'Sam has been violent in the past towards people in authority'*.

Exercise

1. Decide what each of the above statements means to you and then discuss your interpretations with a colleague.

Some forms, in particular those requesting a resource such as day care provision etc., ask 'Is there a history of violence? If "yes" please describe'. How many times in your agency is this section either left blank or given a cursory tick?

Occasionally agencies use a red tag or other system of highlighting the file to indicate that the client has a history of violence. Unfortunately, if the highlight is based upon poor and imprecise information, clients may be unfairly stereotyped and consequently, unfairly dealt with.

There is no excuse for violence. However, its cause or any triggers which give rise to it, must be considered in your assessment of future contact with the client. For example, consider the difference between a one-off provoked incident where the person concerned 'snapped' under heavy emotional pressure and an unprovoked severe assault. Without adequate recording, both will carry the same stigma and will evoke, at least initially, a similar response from anyone seeing the highlight.

The manager's task is clear, s/he must ensure that files are appropriately and adequately completed as well as any other documentation.

Exercise

1. Find any file in which violence has been noted. From the information contained within can you determine the type, severity and form of the violence? Can you identify any contributory factors? The method(s) used to defuse the violence? Do you have a clear description of behaviour? Do you know what started it off? What form it took? What happened afterwards?

Attitudes

Men occupy approximately 70% of management positions in Great Britain. This male dominance in senior positions can influence the culture of the organization, particularly where the male characteristics of aggressive competition, and 'the macho man' approach are considered more dynamic and useful to the organization than sensitive and caring characteristics. This, in turn, can have a direct impact upon the way a unit/organization:

- responds to acts of violence
- views the part played in any incident by the work member.

Often workers can feel doubly abused – first by the aggressor and then by the way the incident is investigated by the organization. It is important to consider how the incident occurred as a way of ensuring that the number of future incidents are minimized. However, management's responsibility must be to ensure that the worker views the investigation as 'fair' and supportive rather than focused on finding fault with the staff member's practice.

There will be an abundance of blame and guilt being experienced already by the victim without it being added to via:

- ill-conceived questions: *'Yes, but just what did you do?'*, or *'but why did you say that?'*
- uninformed responses: *'You must have said or done something, this sort of thing just doesn't happen without provocation of some sort'*
- statements of comparison: *'It's strange how this sort of thing never happens to . . .'*
- indirect criticism: *'This is the second time this has happened to you'*, or *'just how come it always happens to be you who gets it?'*

Reporting incidents

There is a great discrepancy between reported and unreported violent incidents. The reasons given for this reluctance to report violence include:

- not wanting to be identified as a person who 'failed' to handle the situation
- fear of damaging repercussions for the perpetrator
- fear of the incident report appearing in personal files and adversly influencing chances of promotion
- inappropriate responses by managers
- the work culture of bravado which does not allow for the discussion of feelings
- lack of a clearly identified definition of what constitutes 'violence'
- lack of awareness of agency policy regarding reporting of such incidents
- fear of being viewed negatively by colleagues.

It is part of the role of the manager to ensure 'safe working practices' (Health and Safety at Work Act) and this includes enabling staff to report all violent incidents. This is necessary so that a clear picture of their frequency is obtained and action can be taken to reduce the risk of violent incidents reoccurring.

However a number of factors make this part of the management task difficult. Some managers simply do not have the skills or the ability to enable staff to discuss their feelings. Some are uncomfortable with this aspect of their job and a number still believe it is simply not necessary as 'they'll get over it by themselves'.

Many managers will have been through the process of facing violent and aggressive situations during their time as workers. Unfortunately, a number of these may maintain that if they coped with it then so should their staff. Reported incidents therefore tend to be automatically written off as inappropriate, or inadequate handling by the member of staff. However, what is often not considered, is the fact that the job now being done by the worker bears little resemblance to that previously done by the manager. The job has evolved, the pressures have increased and often the resources to deal with these pressures have been reduced.

A proportion of managers may have experienced extreme levels of violence, without the opportunity of any form of debriefing. This poor response by their manager at the time could form a barrier to their effectiveness in dealing with their own staff who later experience a violent incident. Some may re-experience long-held and repressed emotions about their own experience which can come to the fore, while others may retain a certain amount of anger towards a system which effectively failed them and which they then express either overtly or covertly towards their members of staff.

Exercise

1. Think about a violent incident in which you were involved. What questions could have been asked, and in what manner, to help you to discuss the episode?

2. How could the situation in which you were involved have been fairly investigated?

3. Make a list of non-accusatory questions to be asked of any victim following a violent incident which will allow for a fair and supportive investigation of the incident.

Policy statements from management

Many organizations, whose staff encounter violence and aggression on a regular basis, have no policy statements, no guidelines and no advice to offer their staff. Staff are only made aware of what they may, or may not, expect once the episode has taken place and this is often expressed in terms of what the staff member should not have done.

Failure to produce a policy statement will allow for individual responses on the part of managers and rather than encouraging the concept that violence is unacceptable some managers will retain the view that 'it's all a part of the job.'

Staff at all levels within an organization should be given clear and concise guidelines regarding violent and aggressive behaviour. This will then form the basis of the management and prevention of violence within the organization.

The following statements may form the basis of your own working document.
This organization:
- will not tolerate violent behaviour
- will adopt preventive measures to reduce violence towards employees
- will take threats against employees seriously
- will monitor violence to staff as a method of identifying dangerous areas of work
- will take positive sanctions against perpetrators of violence
- will provide training on issues of violence
- will provide legal support, personal injury insurance cover and compensation for victims of violence
- will ensure that prompt and comprehensive support is available to any employee subjected to violence
- will not automatically assume that the employee mishandled the situation
- will acknowledge that managers and staff have a joint responsibility for ensuring safety at work
- will initiate measures for dealing with potentially violent persons
- will encourage a culture where it is considered appropriate, and not a weakness, to acknowledge fear and/or anxiety about a situation and/or person receiving a service from the organization.

In order for these statements to have any value it becomes necessary to give them some substance and in some instances this may mean a resource commitment. Take for example the statement 'will ensure that prompt and comprehensive support is available to any employee subjected to violence'. The resource commitments here may include the employment of a Staff Counsellor, financing private counselling for staff who have experienced violence or training staff to take on an additional 'staff counselling' role.

Exercise

1. From the list given identify how your organization would formulate a working policy on violence towards staff.

15

Gender Issues

The following are a number of statements and questions which may help you to focus on gender issues and the way they may affect the handling of violence. The expectation is that you will find your own solutions to these questions. They are by no means comprehensive and in discussing them with your colleagues, or simply by thinking about them, many more questions should be raised.

1. When confronted by an aggressive person consider what different body signals, postures and behaviours are given by:
   - a female recipient of the aggression?
   - a male recipient of the aggression?

2. Individually, consider:
   - how many times when you have been confronted by an aggressive person have you called on the big, burly, male worker to sort it out for you?
   - how many times have you made basic assumptions that your bear-sized colleague can 'handle himself', and the aggressor, without actually discussing it with him?
   - and by doing this, how many times have you forced your colleague into a role which perhaps he did not want?

3. As a group discuss:
   - when a female worker visits the home of a person with a known history of violence should she take a male colleague with her?
   - when a female worker requests a male colleague to sit in on a potentially dangerous interview what is his role and at what point does he intercede, if at all?

4. You visit the home of a female client and after being invited in discover that her cohabitee has returned. They have obviously been arguing and as you walk into the lounge he stands up and slaps her face in front of you. He then looks towards you with a cynical smirk on his face, his lips curled. Your client, meanwhile, runs from the room into the kitchen on the opposite side of the lounge. Individually or in three groups (one all male, one all female and one mixed) answer the following:
   - what would you be feeling?

- what would you do next and why?

- what would be the possible consequences of your actions?

5. Touch can be used as a therapeutic tool. However it must not be automatically assumed to be of value.
    - Brainstorm those occasions when touch may be used.
    - Brainstorm those occasions when touch may not be used.

6. It is perfectly acceptable for a female colleague to acknowledge that she has been affected by a violent incident. Yet in many workplaces for a male member of staff the converse of this rule holds true. Discuss.

7. Which of the following statements do you agree with:
    - men are taught it is a weakness to show their feelings
    - women are regarded as vulnerable
    - men are viewed as protectors
    - women are 'creatures of emotion'
    - men have different ways of dealing with their emotions from women
    - women talk openly about feelings
    - men are not encouraged to talk about feelings
    - women are encouraged to be sensitive
    - men are taught to 'grin and bear it'
    - women are allowed to cry.

Exercise

1. Do you need to address any of these statements?

2. Which of these statements need to be addressed within your workplace?

8. Individually consider:
   - what would be your reaction(s) if, following a meeting with a client, a male colleague whom you previously regarded as emotionally strong suddenly began to cry?

9. Male managers can actually reinforce the abuse felt by female workers. Discuss how this can occur and suggest ways of ensuring this does not happen within your place of employment.

10. Join with a group of fellow workers to discuss:
    - within any work setting 'male' attitudes contribute to the occurrence of violence and affect its severity.

11. Use the following headings to list any attitudes within your workplace which you feel may have contributed to violent incidents.

Person	Attitude	Expressed by	Outcome

Example:

Person	Attitude	Expressed by	Outcome
David	*Blasé approach*	*'I can handle it'* *Little or no preparation*	*Situation escalated*

Decide how you would constructively address these attitudes with the person expressing them.

16

Summary of Advice

- You do not have to stay. You are not responsible for anothers' actions.
- Arrange to see the person at another time.
- Keep your voice calm and even.
- Do not shout or raise your voice.
- Lower your voice.
- Make no sudden movements.
- Let colleagues know where you are going and when you intend to return.
- Do not point at the aggressor.
- It is easier to run wearing flat shoes.
- A loose tie can be easily grabbed.
- Long, dangly earrings can be grabbed and pulled through pierced ears.
- Tie long hair back.
- Do not give a cigarette to a potential aggressor – it is a possible weapon.
- Heavy glass ashtrays in reception areas can be used as projectiles.
- Have a policy on violence. Use it.
- Be polite and objective.
- Control your own anxiety.
- Do not be blasé, particularly if you know the person.
- Try to distract before becoming involved.
- Break the process of freezing.
- Do not signal 'victim'.
- Sit down.
- Establish eye contact but do not stare.
- Do not ignore the person.
- Walk in a lighted area.
- Carry a personal alarm readily available.
- Practise the techniques outlined.
- Give the person space.
- Give the person respect.
- Do not stand by windows, particularly if the aggressor is now outside.
- Build on the self-esteem of the aggressor.
- Remind the aggressor of past successes.
- Do not take undue risks.
- Take someone with you if the person is not known, has a history of violence, or if you are removing liberty or removing a possession.
- Call the police. Before an incident is better than after.
- Determine a policy for dealing with drunken people or people under the influence of solvents or drugs.
- Allow the aggressor a way out.

- Think about the installation of panic buttons in appropriate places.
- Light porches, car parks and walkways wherever possible.
- Take threats seriously and do something about them.
- Anticipate high risk situations and plan intervention.
- Do not patronize.
- Do not make ultimatums you cannot enforce.
- If you threaten sanctions carry them out.
- After the incident do not assume it is over.
- Renegotiate the relationship.
- If you attend a self-defence course go on refresher courses periodically.
- If people are fighting call the police, remove others in your care from the area.
- Furniture is replaceable. You are not. Better that an interview room is wrecked than you are damaged.

Exercise

1. In a group brainstorm and identify the things you do which wind-up your clients.

The list you arrive at will probably look something like this:
- ignore them altogether
- talk across them to another person
- shout out personal details about them in a room full of others
- dismiss what they are saying
- lie to them
- keep them waiting
- fail to apologize
- deny their importance
- make them look or feel small
- humiliate them
- give them indifferent attention
- wear a smirk
- wag a finger.

This list, or your list which may contain other elements more appropriate to your setting, must now be regarded as a list of *do not's* particularly when dealing with an aggressive or potentially aggressive person.

17

Case Studies

These case studies are provided for use at any stage throughout this workbook. They are focused mainly on situations facing social workers, however they can be altered to suit situations more appropriate to your own work. Please read the case studies carefully and answer the questions before going on to the discussion and presentations.

Case study A

It is late Friday evening one November. Most people have gone home already. The place is becoming dark as the lights are switched off by different people as they leave. You are probably not alone in the building but it certainly feels like it. As you walk past the locker room you hear a noise and decide to investigate. You walk into the room putting the lights on as you do so and see a body curled up in the far corner. He says pleadingly, *'Not the lights, please,'* and hearing the pleading in his voice you switch them off again. You have recognized the young man as being a new client at the centre. He is a 20-year old man, stockily-built who has a history of being in and out of various hostels and hospitals since he was seriously abused by his parents as a child. You know that he had been involved in an heated argument earlier in the evening with another client at the centre, but you thought that he had gone home after storming out immediately following the shouting match. You go over to see how he is and kneel by him. You are about to touch him compassionately when he springs up shouting, *'You're just like all the rest'*. He stands over you, his shoulders hunched and starts to threaten he will *'do you!'*

1. How would you feel?

2. What would be your first action?

3. What would be your second action?

4. What would you say and how would you say it?

Group task

1. Compare, and discuss, your answers within your group and agree upon a way of handling this situation.

2. Decide on an imaginative method of feeding back the way your group would handle the situation.

Case study B

Name: Mr James Henry Whittaker
Address: 52 Elm Court, Manor Park Estate, Anytown.
Age/DoB: 76 years 2.3.13
GP: Dr McManus, 22 Home Park Road, Anytown.
Reason for referral: General assessment requested by GP.

Information

Mr Whittaker was widowed approximately two years ago after a long and happy marriage. His wife, Elsie, had been ill for the latter part of her life and had required considerable care and attention which Henry gave. Now however, Henry has begun to neglect himself. He is not eating regularly. Although he does seem to purchase food most is simply left to rot in his kitchen. The home, originally very clean and well kept by Henry while his wife was living, is now described by the GP as 'uncared for and somewhat dirty'. Neighbours have complained about the smell.

Apparently Henry has begun to frequent public houses and the GP feels he is drinking heavily because he has little to occupy him. He is in severe rent arrears. His health is beginning to suffer because he is apparently failing to eat. The request is for a general assessment and offer of appropriate intervention/facilities etc.

The couple had few friends as they preferred each other's company. A son, Charles, his wife and child were killed in a car accident in 1965. There is no other known family. The home is a fifth floor flat in a run down area in the borough. Throughout the flat Mr Whittaker keeps a variety of photographs of his wife and himself, and his son and family on show.

1. What plans would you make for an initial visit?

2. You decide to go alone to visit. You knock on the door and after a while it is opened by a small, partly bent, frail-looking old man. You explain why you are there and he invites you in. You smell alcohol on his breath. What would you do next and why?

3. You decide to go in and walk into the lounge. The place is like a tip. The furniture cluttered and grimy. You hear the door banged shut behind you and as you turn around the old man is standing in the doorway. He lifts his stick and waves it at you and angrily shouts, *'What yer doin' here pokin' yer nose in?'*. What would you do next and why?

Case study C

Name: David Charles Bray
Age: 39
Address: 22 Charlworth Court, Albany Park Estate, Anytown.
Reason for referral to centre: To attempt to break the frequency of hospital admissions. To offer support to the family by allowing breaks from each other.

Information

Mr Bray suffered what was termed by his parents a 'breakdown' seven years ago. He was previously a technician with British Transporters Ltd, and was responsible for running a large section including 23 staff and a budget of £½ million. While at work he began to hear voices telling him what he did was morally wrong. He became obsessed with the idea that God had chosen him to bring about change to the world and began to systematically sabotage his and his colleagues work. Finally he was dismissed from his position when he attacked a female worker.

Later that same year Mr Bray was admitted to a mental hospital under section 29, later changed to section 25 and eventually section 60. He was an in-patient for almost four months initially and was diagnosed as suffering from a 'personality disorder with schiziod overtones'. He was discharged home on medication and has been in and out of hospital ever since. His behaviour is described as moody and unpredictable.

Mr Bray lives with his parents, Sarah and David Bray who are aged 67 and 69 years. He is an only child. The parents blame themselves for their son's behaviour and trace it to an incident which occurred in his childhood (at aged 7 approximately) when they played hide and seek with him. They told him that he must not be found as they were Jews and he would be put in a concentration camp. He remained hidden from them for two days, later being found in the cellar. Ever since this time he has expressed a feeling of isolation and fear. The family are not Jewish.

Although blaming themselves, both parents find their son's behaviour distressing and unacceptable, and displace their anger scathingly on authority figures. The family have moved three times in the last seven years.

Situation to date

You have visited Mr Bray at home on two occasions and have accompanied him to the centre once. His parents are frustrated that the move to the day centre is going so slowly, having seen your role as being one of arranging admission. You visit today. You walk into the lounge, having passed the stairway. Mr Bray senior has a black eye and Mrs Bray blames you for it *'for being so slow in arranging everything'*. She insists you *'do something'* as *'he's stopped taking his tablets'*. Upstairs you hear David chanting rhythmically. Then you hear him coming downstairs.

1. What would be your plan to reduce the possibility of violence occurring?

Case study D

You have just seen a distressed resident downstairs. David Harris was weeping because of an argument he had just had with another resident (Billy Mears) in a pub. You make him a cup of tea and he goes to bed, but leaves his cup at the top of the stairs. You collect the empty cup, and walk down the stairs. You can hear the television from the lounge downstairs and somebody making supper in the kitchen. You hear a noise and realize that the front door was left on the latch and it is now being opened. At the foot of the stairs is a very aggressive-looking, irate and unkempt Billy Mears. He has obviously been drinking, although still on his medication, and sways a little as he looks up and sees you.

'Where's the f...... bastard!' he demands pointing at you. 'Where is he?' he shouts, 'I'll teach him.' As he starts to walk towards you up the stairs you notice he is carrying a half-empty bottle of whisky. His face is white and drawn, his eyes fixed and focused upon you. 'You'll not stop me. I'll kill the f...... bastard', he almost shouts. You hear a sound behind you and realize that David has heard the commotion.

Individual task

Please complete the following questions as fully as possible.
1. How would you feel?

2. What would be your first action?

3. What would be your second action?

Group task

1. Discuss your answers within the group and then determine an appropriate way of dealing with the situation to ensure that the possibility of violence is minimized.

2. Feedback to the whole group imaginatively the way you would handle the situation.

Case study E

It is early Friday evening. You are on duty with one other worker. You receive a message from the police – David Morrison has been picked up. He is being held in the cells where he has already been for about one hour. The police say he is very frightened and has wrapped himself up in a blanket and is in the corner of the cell weeping. He is 14 years old and has been missing for three days. Night duty say they cannot pick him up because of other priorities and cannot guarantee to collect tomorrow.

David has been with you for a period of assessment. You are his key worker. You feel you know him very well. He comes from a family where violence is a common occurrence. He is unable to build meaningful relationships and has a history of outbursts of anger against his father, male teachers and other male figures. He is in care as a result of 'an uncontrollable outburst' in school where he assaulted a teacher. He is 4' 6'' tall and described as 'lanky with self-imposed tattoos on his hands and arms, a very strong lad particularly when under the influence of solvents'. He ran away from care following a fight which occurred after three other children started to bait him about his parents. You were not on duty at the time and feel the situation was mishandled by the staff members present, one of whom is on duty with you tonight. You still have some feelings about this.

David has been the subject of abuse since his early years. He was frequently hit by his father and locked away for days in a garden shed, often in winter, for failing to do something requested of him. He has a poor self-image, has self-inflicted wounds and has a minor history of solvent abuse. The police say they think he has been sniffing today but he is quiet now.

1. As the key worker what would you do next and why?

Case study F

Name: Sarah Pollock
Address: 32 Aldringham Crescent, Newtown.
DoB/Age: 2.4.48
GP: Dr Weightam, The Hollies, Sandringham Park Road, Newtown.

Home circumstances

Miss Pollock lives with her parents in a terraced row of town houses. The family recently moved to this address from Wandsworth, London and have been in the area for three months. Dr Weightam has only seen the family on two previous occasions. Both parents reside at the address: father – Peter Pollock, aged 67 years, retired prison warder; mother – Rachel Mary Pollock, aged 64 years, housewife; subject – Sarah Pollock, unemployed. Information provided by Dr Weightam.

Presenting problem

Mr and Mrs Pollock informed Dr Weightam that Sarah had a history of 'mental outbursts' when her behaviour could be unpredictable although they feel she will not harm anyone. She has had a number of admissions to a psychiatric hospital in Wandsworth, London (Mayfield Hospital).

Yesterday Sarah began shouting and screaming in her room. She threw a bottle of perfume at a park-keeper who was passing outside and became uncontrollable. Her parents have not entered her room for three to four days as she refused to let them in. Food is left on the stairs for her. Dr Weightam called yesterday and was unable to gain entry into her room. He arranged for a psychiatric assessment which took place this morning. Although they were unable to gain entry to her room, both GP and psychiatrist felt she was a danger to herself, possibly to others and that she needed to receive treatment. She is insisting that agents are about to arrest her and her family. Medical recommendation forms have been completed and left with the parents.

Action required

Assessment by ASW expressed by GP as identification that bed is available on Willow Ward. Time: 3.00 pm. Day: Friday.
1. Complete assessment ensuring potential for violence is minimized.

Case study G

Name: David James Rider, known as Jimmy
DoB: 25.1.76
Address: 14 Charlworth House, Eastlands Estate.
School: Abbotsbury Manor

Problem

Jimmy has been missing more and more lessons, particularly towards the end of the day and in the early morning. On arrival (late most mornings) he has been described as 'sleepy', 'yawning', 'scruffy and unkempt' and 'dirty' by different school teachers. Headmaster, Mr Jarrot and form teacher Mrs Pollit say they are unable to find out what is wrong. They have sent letters to the parents but these have apparently been ignored. They have also tried talking with the boy but he is sullen and 'uncommunicative'.

Last week Jimmy was absent for the majority of lessons and when he finally did show up on Friday (standing outside the school gates watching the other children playing) he was smelly and unwashed and gave every impression he had slept rough for a couple of nights. When questioned he ran off.

Referral for assessment of home circumstances and possible intervention.

Home circumstances

Charlworth House is a medium/high rise block in a run-down area. Both parents are living at home, and both are unemployed. Other information from neighbours suggests that Mr Rider drinks heavily and there are apparently frequent shouting bouts, if not fights involving both parents.

Jimmy has been at Abbotsbury Manor School for only two terms. Records from his previous school (Belmont, Woolwich) went missing en-route. Jimmy was removed from SSD's At Risk register prior to moving from his previous address. The relevant information is still to arrive in your office.

1. What would you do and why?

2. You visit the home and are greeted by Mrs Rider. She has a black eye. After explaining who you are she reluctantly invites you in, but insists that you keep your voice to a whisper, as her husband is asleep after returning from the pub.
    - What would you do and why?

3. You go in. The place is a mess. Jimmy is asleep, still in his clothes, on the couch. It is late morning. Mrs Rider grabs him harshly and hauling him to his feet shouts *'Look what you've done. You've got the authorities at me.'* From the other room a gruff voice shouts, *'What the f . . . s going on?'*
   - What would you do?

4. Mr Rider enters and starts shouting. He goes to his wife and pushes her to the couch. Jimmy places himself between his mother and his father and is clouted around the ear by Mr Rider.
   - What would you do and why?

5. Discuss your answers and choose either questions 2, 3 or 4 (or a combination) and provide an imaginative feedback session for discussion by the whole group.

Bibliography

1. *Preventing Violence to Staff*, HMSO
2. *Violence to Staff: report of the DHSS Advisory Committee on violence to staff*, HMSO (1988)
3. *Violence to Staff in the Health Services*, HMSO (1986)
4. Poyner B and Warne C, *Violence to Staff: a basis for assessment and prevention*, Health and Safety Executive, HMSO
5. *Violence to Staff*, Health and Safety Executive (1989)
6. *Guidelines and Recommendations to Employers on Violence Against Employees in the Personal Social Services*, Association of Directors of Social Services (1987)
7. *Violence in Libraries*, Library Association (1987)
8. *The Cost of Violence*, Local Government Training Board Seminar Report (April 1988)
9. Heining D, Workers at Risk, *Social Work Today* (19.7.1990)
10. Braithwaite R, Drawing Out the Fear, *Social Work Today* (19.7.1990)
11. Clarke S and Kidd B, Part of the Job, *Social Work Today* (19.7.1990)
12. *Guidance to Staff on Violence by Clients*, Cheshire Social Services
13. *Coping With Violence*, Royal Borough of Kingston-upon-Thames (1990)
14. C Rowett, *Violence in Social Work* (1986)
15. Braithwaite R, Coming to Terms with the Effects of Violence, *Social Work Today* (20.10.1988)
16. Braithwaite R, Creating a Place of Solace, *Community Care* (27.10.1988)
17. Phillips R and Leadbetter D, Violent Sessions in the Classroom, *Social Work Today* (1.2.1990)
18. Tumelty D, Lessons of Piper Alpha, *Social Work Today* (1.2.1990 and 8.2.1990)
19. Stewart M, Mirrors of Pain: helping in disasters, *Community Care* (2.2.1989)
20. Braithwaite R, Training for Trouble, *Community Care* (27.7.1989)
21. Lamplugh D, *Beating Aggression: a practical guide for working women*, Weidenfield and Nicholson (1988)

Video material

1. A training video by Ray Braithwaite (in association with the Home Office), on violence and aggression will be available later in the year.
2. *Look Closer: see me*. This looks at aggression and the elderly. Local Government Training Board, Arndale House, Arndale Centre, Luton LU1 ETS. Tel: 0582 451166
3. *On the Front Line*. For staff who have face to face contact with the public. Local Government Training Board (see above)
4. *Avoiding Danger*. Designed to help avoid the risk of personal attacks at work. The Suzy Lamplugh Trust, 14 East Sheen Avenue, London SW14 8AS

Index